All My Love, George...

Letters from a WWII Hero

Darla Noble

Dedication

To my husband, John-you are the love of my life. Your dedication to our family makes it possible for me to write.

To Dad-I hope in writing this book others will come to know Uncle George for the fun-loving, kind, gentle, and heroic young man he was.

To Zach, Elizabeth, Olivia, and Emma — you are the best thing I've ever done in my life. No mother could ask for more.

To Uncle George. I wish we could have known one another because the man I have come to know through your letters and in talking to Dad is someone I deeply love and respect.

Foreword

The physical and emotional battles brave American men and women have fought to protect the freedoms of our great nation have been immortalized both on screen and in the pages of books from a number of perspectives. Parents, wives or girlfriends, sons and daughters, and even the soldiers themselves have given us a glimpse into the lives of both returning and fallen heroes. They have opened their hearts and souls to us, sharing their grief, their memories, and most importantly, their respect, dedication, and admiration for this country.

But what about a soldier's siblings? Has anyone ever given much thought about what it would be like to be the one staring across the dinner table at the empty seat once occupied by an older brother or sister? Or considered how it feels to lie down each night knowing that the bed on the other side of the room or down the hall is empty — and is going to stay that way? Has anyone really given much thought to how a younger brother or sister works through their grief when that dreaded news comes in the form of a knock at the door and a telegram?

I have, because my father, Grover Bentley (Benny) Burks is one of those siblings. He is the reason for this book, which is a tribute to an older brother he loved, respected, and lost.

Out of the blue a few years ago, Dad said he wanted to share some things with me; things belonging to his older brother, George. I had grown up hearing the name Uncle George. I knew he was one of my dad's older brothers and that he had died in WW II. I knew we had the flag that had been draped over his coffin and the telegram telling my grandparents (and my father) their son (and brother) had died in combat. I knew his was the grave next to my grandparents' and that we put flowers on it each Memorial Day. But I didn't have a clue as to who he really was; what he liked to do or what kind of brother he'd been.

I am also ashamed to say that I had never given any thought as to how my father felt about the fact that he had lost a brother so tragically or that a member of our family had died a hero. I had never thought about how, as a child, my dad had experienced the pain of losing a much-loved older brother.

So why, after nearly seventy years, would Dad have something to show me? And what could it be? The 'what' was an old beat-up black metal box Dad took down off a shelf in a bedroom closet. It was the box which held letters my uncle had written home, pictures he'd sent and other mementos (Purple Hearts, a Silver Star, and a commendation for a Distinguished Service Cross). Looking inside the box was like stepping back in time to the 1940's. The 'why' is a bit more complicated but can best be explained by simply saying it was time.

We both looked inside the box silently for a few seconds before Dad started talking about the day he and my grandparents took George to the bus station to leave for boot camp. It was also the last time they saw him.

Almost speaking more to himself than to me, there was unmistakable pain in my father's voice. I was mesmerized by what he was saying and emotionally transported back in time. I knew immediately that I needed to do something to help preserve Uncle George's memory; something that would hopefully ease the pain still lingering in Dad's heart after all these years. I just wasn't sure in the moment what that something would be.

It didn't take long to decide, though, and this book is that something. This book is a tribute to the older brother my father loved and admired and to the young man whose kind heart and gentle spirit were willingly sacrificed for our freedom. This book has been written to tell my dad how much I love him and how sorry I am for his loss. It was also written that we might remember a time when so many gave so much. It is a picking up of the gauntlet, so to speak, so that their pain, suffering and death will not have been for nothing.

What you are about to read are George's letters home to my grandparents and my dad, coupled with my father's memories of those days long ago and his thoughts and feelings about the older brother he loved and admired so much. Additionally, you will find important historical facts pertaining to the campaign in the South Pacific during World War II, which are interjected where necessary to put everything into perspective.

Thanks, Dad, for answering all the hard questions it took to make this book possible. Thanks for being willing to relive the memories; both the pleasant and the painful, so that we can all know and hopefully not forget.

A Leader In
Animal Nutrition Since 1912

When no news is good news

"We knew. We didn't have to open the telegram. We didn't even need the telegram. The look on the face of the men in uniform standing at our door was enough to let Mom and I know that George was gone."

"Yes, it really did happen that way-the way it happens in the movies. The telegram informing you that your loved one is either dead or missing in action is delivered to you in person. Yes, a real person hands it to you but there is no personal warmth or interaction. If I had to choose a word to describe it, I think that word would be mechanical."

"I hadn't been home from school very long that day when they arrived. I still remember thinking how glad I was that Mom hadn't been alone when she'd gotten the news. I was fourteen and the only one of us kids left at home. But that was plenty old enough to feel my own pain and know I couldn't possibly understand hers."

"I did what I could, though. I remember putting my hand on her shoulder when she sat down (dropped into) in the chair. She was shaking so badly. It took her a while to bring herself to open the envelope."

"I can still remember how I could feel her shoulder shaking under my hand when she finally took a big, deep breath and slid her finger underneath the edge of the envelope. But it wasn't until after she actually read the words printed on that telegram that the tears came-both hers and mine."

"Somehow I managed to go ahead and do my chores. Mom probably insisted-thinking the distraction would help pass the time until Dad came home. As I milked and fed the cow and gathered the eggs, I remember feeling like it wasn't real and that when Dad got home everything would be ok. It wasn't."

"Dad was a feed and tobacco salesman and spent a lot of time driving from store to store servicing his customers. The stores he went to were scattered around the little communities in Miller and Pulaski counties in Missouri where I grew up. There was no way to get a hold of him so he could come home early. We just had to wait. Thinking about it just now, I feel so sorry for Mom. I wonder how many times she went over and over in her mind just how she would tell Dad about the telegram-or if she even would. Maybe she would just hand it to him."

"As it turned out she didn't have to do either. He could tell the minute he walked through the door that we had received a piece of paper that turned my family's life upside down."

"The days immediately following are vague. Mom and Dad did not make me go to school the next day. Dad did go to work, though. I think. I honestly don't remember. What I do remember is feeling strange-like I was on the outside of my life looking in. I remember my older sisters and brothers calling a couple of times a day to check on Dad and Mom."

"It was especially hard for my sister, Helen. It had been only a few months since my brother-in-law, Charles, had died while serving in PNG (Papa New Guinea). Losing Charles had been hard enough. Why did we have to lose George, too? And where in the world was Luzon? I'd never even heard of such a place."

"I also remember that when I did go back to school a couple of days later, it took everything I had to try to feel and act normal. I remember thinking I wasn't sure how to act. Would anyone understand that things were different in my life now? Would anyone understand that my brother was dead?"

"I told some of my buddies, but I think they already knew. Most everyone had heard the news. Crocker, MO is a small town and the saying about news traveling fast in a small town is true. Some of my classmates said things like 'I'm sorry about your brother' or 'George was a great guy'. Some of the teachers told me to pass on their sympathies to my parents and others told me I could be proud that George died a hero. I'd heard that already. It was in the telegram we'd received, but I have to say that I didn't want George to be a hero. I wanted him to be alive."

"One of the first-grade teachers at school was one of Dad's cousins and I remember her giving me a hug and telling me she was sorry about what had happened to George. For some reason, her words meant the most. I think it was because she'd known George all of his life-she was family. I also remember her asking when the funeral would be."

"Funeral? What funeral? There wouldn't be one…not for three long years, anyway. And even then you have to wonder if it was only a box. Dad didn't want to believe it was, but his gut instinct told him it probably was. As for me, I refused to think that was even possible. The army wouldn't lie about something like that, would they?"

"The teenager who'd lost his big brother didn't comprehend the complexities of trying to return a loved one's remains during WWII or the fact that in tens of thousands of cases, the impossibility of doing so."

"That is why a loved one's remains were sent only if you requested it and since we were in the middle of a war, it wasn't on the top of the army's list of things to do."

"I know that sounds harsh, but you have to remember there were 406,000 Americans killed overseas and in Pearl Harbor during WWII. Many of those who died were identified only by the dog tags because nothing else was left or identifiable. The letter we got said that George's remains was buried in a military cemetery over there-in Manila (the Philippines). They even sent a picture of the grave. That wasn't enough, though."

"Dad and Mom wanted, no, *needed* something more. We just did not have any idea when that would happen. As it turns out, it would be more than three long years."

"In the meantime, though, we didn't have any choice but to get on with life. Dad went to work every day, Mom took care of us and the house, and I went to school, did my chores, had a paper route and all of the other things a young boy did growing up in a rural community in the '40's."

"The war ended a few months after George died, and we moved from Crocker to Rolla, MO about a year after that. But life was never the same. It got easier, but never the same. There were even times when I felt guilty for feeling happy."

"Moving in the middle of my sophomore year in high school would be considered a fate worse than death to most kids that age these days, but I don't recall being the least bit upset. I'm sure one reason for my attitude was simply the fact that I respected and obeyed my parents. Thinking or telling them they were ruining my life didn't even cross my mind. But at the center of it all was the fact that Dad, Mom, and I all were grateful for the change. Moving meant we could remember George without being able to see him sitting at his place at the table or tinkering on a car with Dad in the garage."

"I graduated from high school in the spring of 1948 and was getting ready to go to college when we received notice that Dad would need to be at the train station on July 9th to claim George's remains. That's right…George died on March 23, 1945, but we didn't receive that flag-draped coffin until July 9th, 1948."

"Why so long? Why did we have to go through this again? I didn't want to feel all those feelings again. NOT because I didn't want to remember George; I thought about George every single day. I still missed him terribly. Time had just made it a different kind of 'missing'; one that was more sweet than bitter. I didn't want to go back to the bitter."

"I hated it for Dad and Mom, too. I can't begin to imagine how I would be able to go through all of that if it were one of you kids. I honestly don't know how Dad and Mom did it."

FYI

George E. Burks served with the United States Army from 1942 until he was killed in action in March of 1945; reaching the rank of Technician 3rd Grade (equivalent to a staff sergeant). He served as a medic with the 43rd Division of the 103rd Infantry. The 43rd was nicknamed the "Winged Victory" even though they were a ground unit. The 43rd was established during the Revolutionary War and was a highly respected fighting unit until it was disbanded in October of 1945 following their return from the South Pacific.

George and his fellow soldiers fought hard and proud. During their tour in the South Pacific, the men collectively were awarded the following:

- 4 Presidential Unit Citations
- 2 Medal of Honor recipients
- 40 Distinguished Service Cross recipients (George was one of them)
- 736 Silver Star Medal recipients (George was one of them)
- 53 Legion of Merit recipients
- 51 Soldiers Medal recipients
- 2,496 Bronze Star Medal recipients (George was one of them)
- 27 Air Medal recipients

- Undetermined number of Purple Heart recipients (George was one of them)

August 25, 1942

Dear Dad,

Just got in from two days out. We left yesterday morning, arrived at our destination about 11a. We had classes yesterday afternoon and this morning. I got a very nice view of the river last night as we passed by it on a hike we had.

The army keeps you busy! The river here is about the size of the Mo (Missouri River) at Jefferson City. We slept in pup tents they are just about big enough for 2 fellows to sleep in. Two people put them up too.

The food was very good. Of course our pies and cakes were cooked at the camp and brought out to us in trucks.

Helen sent me my pen and camera today so I can start sending some pictures home.

Next week we spend two nights in the woods. The following week-which is supposed to be our last one here- we spend three nights out.

I went to the service club in camp Saturday night and watched the big dance for a while.

I doubt if Benny is the only one that is tickled over his dog. School starts Monday and then is when he will have fun when the pup starts to follow him.

Tell everyone hello for me.

With love,

George

"I'll never forget the day we took George to Jefferson City (MO) to catch the train that would take him to boot camp. It was the middle of July. I don't remember much being said on the trip up there from Crocker. Probably things like 'be sure and write', and 'don't forget where you came from'. I'm sure Mom went over some instructions on how to do his laundry and warned him to eat right; idle small talk meant to make us all believe that this was just another family outing"

"I also remember hugging George before he got on the train, and I remember him telling me to be good and to be sure and write with all the news about people at home. I remember Dad and George hanging on to each other for what seemed like a very long time. This would have made some boys my age uncomfortable but I'm sure I didn't think so. Dad was always ready with a hug or a pat on the back and assurances of his pride in each of us kids. Mom was overly solicitous; straightening George's shirt collar, brushing away a stray piece of lint on his shirt and patting him on the arm. I promised to keep him up to date on how the high school basketball team did. George had been the star of the team when he was in high school and still loved to keep up with them."

"When it was time for George to leave I remember watching him get on the train. Dad and Mom's eyes were tear-filled. I had a huge lump in my throat that wouldn't go down. I remember wondering when we would see him again, but it never entered my mind that there wouldn't be an 'again'-that this would be the last time I would ever see George. I've wondered now and then if I would have said or done anything differently if I would have known. The answer is always 'no'. George and I were ten years apart in age, but we were close. He knew long before I told him that day at the train station that I loved him. Besides, what else would a twelve-year-old know to say?"

"We waited on the platform until the train was out of sight before heading back to the car to make the sixty-mile drive home. As we drove down Monroe Street heading out of town, I remember looking out the back window long after I could see the train station from the rear window."

"Little did I know that day at the train station I would end up living here in Jefferson City. I've lived here almost sixty years and to this day I still haven't driven down that part of Monroe Street and I've not gone to the train station. Not even once."

"George mentioned our dog, Buster. What a dog! He was an Eskimo Husky. He *did* follow me just about everywhere I went, but not to school. Mom kept him inside every morning so he couldn't. If there was anyone he was more protective of than me, it was Mom. Buster was the kind of dog every family needs. Dad and Mom loved that dog as much as I did. George would have loved him, too. I remember sending George a picture of me and Buster together.

"George loved people and was one of the most genuine guys you could ever meet. He loved for us to write about what everyone back home was doing and send pictures of anything from home. He sent pictures of himself and his friends home to us, too, whenever he could. When George asked you how you were, he really wanted to know. He was always interested in how I was doing in school, and what was going on in my life. As a kid I didn't really give it much thought, but the fact that he took the time to ask about his kid brother while he was in the middle of a war says a lot about the man he was. To me he was just being George."

August 31, 1942

Dearest Dad,

Went to a show this afternoon, saw "Mrs. Minevar". It is a wonderful picture-one of the best I've seen. I've been busy around the camp a large part of the day too.

Done a large washing. Rerolled my pack, etc. The laundry service is not too good here. Clothes are not washed too clean and you are not sure you will get your own clothes back.

I am sending a picture. Helen sent me my camera Sat., so I will be sending a lot home by the last of next week.

In case I don't call Monday night, we may have to stay after chow and get paid. By the time this procedure is over it may be too late to call. Will call Thurs. night the third of September at eight o'clock. If I don't call Monday. Dad, if you are planning on coming down be sure and let me know 3-4 days ahead of time. The hotels are jammed here over the weekends.

Had another nice letter from Harold. He seems to have a new slant on everything.

We had a personal inspection yesterday. One of the fellows in E Co. laughed while the C.O. was giving him the 'once over'-just a sudden impulse. It does give you a funny feeling the way they (C.O.'s) look you over.

They pet saying of the non-com's here is 'off and on'. Off your ass, on your feet, out of the shade and into the heat. Almost time for lights out and I still have to shave.

With love,
George

"Helen was one of my oldest sisters. She was really great about sending things to George-like the camera he talked about in this letter. That camera and the other things we sent from home were important to George-they are to any soldier. But out of everything we sent the camera was probably his favorite. He wanted to make sure he'd have something to show us that would help explain what his life was like while he was gone. As it turned out, those pictures and these letters are the only things we have to tell us about George's last years. That camera was his connection to us, and ours to him. At the time, getting the pictures in the mail was exciting to this little country boy. The war effort was first and foremost in everyone's mind and the pictures were a trophy of sorts and proof we were doing our patriotic duty. That's just the way it was back then. Everyone either had at least one family member or a friend in the war. The whole country was involved in the war effort. I know a lot of people don't get that today."

"George was also really close to Helen. When he left Crocker to go to college he lived with Helen and her husband, Charles. Charles-now there was a great guy! He and George were a lot alike. They were both genuine, had hearts as big as they were and never passed me over even though I was just a kid."

"George and I were ten years apart and Charles was old enough to be my dad, but that didn't matter to either of them. Anyway, since Helen had both a brother and her husband serving overseas, anything she could do to make their lives easier was as much a comfort to her as it was to them."

"Phone calls were few and far between. You have to remember that this was long before cell phones were even thought about. A lot of people didn't even have a phone in their house at this point. We did, but I don't remember George calling that night or ever. It could be that I just wasn't home when he did."

"I remember Mom and Dad planned to go to Arkansas to visit George while he was in training there. I think my cousin Inah was going to stay with me. They really wanted to go because they knew that after he left there he would be going to Camp Ord in California and there would be no chance of seeing him until either the war was over, or he got to come home."

"I imagine it was nothing more than life getting in the way, but their plans to visit never materialized. This was 1942. Families were still trying to recover from the Depression so time and money for road trips-no matter how important-were luxuries still hard to come by."

"I don't remember Dad or Mom ever saying, 'if only we would have....' after George was gone, but I know they must have thought about it. Being a parent myself, I know *I* would have. That's just the way it was back then, though."

"Gas was rationed; meaning you were allowed to purchase only the amount of gas deemed absolutely necessary for you to exist. I think because of Dad's job that meant we got up to eight gallons a week. Dad's job as a salesman was mainly pay on commission, so he only got paid for what he sold, and vacation benefits weren't a part of 'the package'. There wasn't even a 'package'."

"In other words, living with the regret of having to concede to life getting in the way was something you just couldn't do. But then, I'm sure the fact that George might not come home wasn't foremost in their minds. It couldn't have been, or it would have driven them crazy."

"George didn't go into detail about what happened to the young soldier who made the mistake of laughing during inspection. He couldn't, but we could read between the lines."

"Knowing George, though, I'm sure he was the first one to offer encouragement to the poor guy. George was never the type to bully or make fun of someone, and he was always concerned about other people."

"You'll see this in the letters he writes while he is overseas. George always wrote of his concern for the safety and health of the people he loved-even though *he* was the one in danger."

May 27, 1943

Dear Benny,

 Received your most welcome letter today. It really saved the day, as I was feeling a bit homesick and your letter was so newsy. I am still in the hospital but expect to return to my outfit in the next few days. I just returned from a ten-day sick leave. They have given me a final checkup and found nothing wrong. So guess I will join the boys and go to work.

 Say, you sure do make a fellow's mouth water talking about fried chicken, spareribs, and kraut. Tell your mother I am looking forward to that fried chicken but also tell her it is hard to play pitch and eat fried chicken. HA!

 Was sorry to hear Inah was ill. When you see them, tell them hello, and tell Inah not to forget how to make those egg custards. She and I have a standing date when I return. I often think of the times when Ralph Madden and I used to slip in and raid Nancy's ice box thinking she wouldn't hear us. HA!

 It is wintertime here now, and it seems odd not to have snow. It never snows here, and their winter weather is just chilly-never gets very cold. In fact, people go swimming in the ocean all winter long. I spent two days of my sick leave at the seashore. It was great fun to ride the big waves when the tide comes in. All you have to do is lie down and they take you back on the beach.

I have made me two daggers out of swords. We have to carry large knives strapped to our belts to cut our way through the jungles. We had a hard time keeping them as the black natives would steal them. They are crazy about knives and will do almost anything for cigarettes or any kind of shiny jewelry or beads. Their chief meat is dog. After they kill them, they make beads out of the teeth. Almost all of them have a string of dog teeth around their neck.

Well Benny, old boy, must say so long for now. Write when you can. Love and best wishes to all.

Your brother,
Charles

"This is obviously not a letter from George. It's a letter from my brother in-law Charles Shular. I've already mentioned that he always treated me like I was his 'real' brother. I wrote him several letters and he always wrote back. I wish I had more of the letters he wrote me because they meant as much to me as the ones George wrote. He didn't have to write, but he did, and it meant a lot to me. It still does. I remember one letter he wrote when he was in the army hospital about us doing something when he got home, but Charles didn't make it home alive, either. He was a medic like George and served in Australia and in the jungles of Papua New Guinea."

"Charles wasn't killed in action, though. He contracted malaria while he was over there. From what his letters said and from what my sister Helen knew, Charles was well on the road to recovery, but insisted on going back to serve with his unit before he really should have been allowed to. That's what he was talking about in this letter when he said he would be heading back to work. Going back too soon caused him to have a relapse and he died. I know Charles, though. I can see him laughing and talking his way into being allowed to go back. He was a hard worker and would never have taken advantage of being sick. I was just a little kid, but even I knew back then that Charles wasn't that kind of guy or soldier."

"If there was anyone who loved Mom's fried chicken more than I did, it was Charles. Dad always said he didn't know of anything he felt sorrier for than a chicken after Charles or I had gotten through with it. Mom, on the other hand, loved the fact that we 'fought' over her cooking. Fighting wasn't necessary, though, because somehow she always made sure there was plenty for all of us."

"There have been more changes than we can count in this world since Charles wrote that letter, but it's nice to know that there are some things never change…fried chicken is still the best meal to be had as far as I'm concerned."

"The reference to playing pitch was for Mom. She and Charles loved the game. They were friendly rivals, you might say. Pitch was to Mom and Charles what fried chicken was to Charles and me. Oh, Charles…he was quite a guy and couldn't have been any more a part of our family if he would have been born into it rather than marry into it. And it was obvious even to me how much he and Helen loved each other. If there was any consolation to be had in his dying so young, it was that he appreciated and loved his family to the fullest and he made the most of every single day he did have here on earth. He took it all in and found the good in everyone and everything."

"I can just see Charles sitting in camp in the middle of a jungle making those daggers. And I can see him trying to joke around with the natives and get on friendly terms with them. Don't get me wrong-there is no doubt in my mind Charles took his job seriously and that he was good at it. He just wasn't the type to pass up the opportunity to experience something as new and different as interacting with such a different group of people. If he weren't dedicated to his job and his duties as a soldier, he would have taken all the sick leave they would give him, and he would have probably made it out of there alive. But he didn't-he put his commitment to his unit above his health and paid for it with his life."

"Charles signed the letter 'Your brother'. Yes, he really was my older brother in every sense of the word. Like I said, he was family. Dad and Mom considered him their son not just the guy who happened to marry their daughter. Charles' death was difficult and painful for all of us. One of us was no longer here and it hurt. It hurt badly enough that even as a kid I knew I didn't want to go through that ever again."

"But by this time George was in the South Pacific, and we knew he'd been involved in major battles over there so Charles' death made the possibility of George not coming back even more real."

"I remember thinking about how real the war and dying was now. And it wasn't nearly as exciting thrilling as the movies made it seem. I knew first-hand that these things really happened to real families in our little spot in the world and that ours was one of those families."

"I don't remember who it was, but I remember when Charles died someone said to us that our family had paid its dues to the war. In the mind I thought that meant George was safe. Surely nothing would happen to him now. Surely the very thing we were going through with Charles we wouldn't have to go through with George…"

"It was several years after his death before Helen remarried and had a family. She was happy, and for that I'm thankful. But I know she never forgot her Charles. Neither will I."

Sept. 1942

Dearest Dad,

Am sorry I didn't write yesterday, but there isn't much to write about out here. I went to the show Sunday night and last night. It wasn't so much that I wanted to see the shows, but it helped to pass away some time.

I haven't done two hours' work since we've been here. The old (in service longer) men have been going out on the range with the regiment for the past few days. There have been times in the past 3 mo. When I wished I was out of the medics. The reason was that as big and healthy as I am, I thought I could be doing something a little harder-something at which you had to work. I now realize that I have one of the hardest jobs of all. That my knowledge and the way I do my job may save someone's life. Most of the fellows that are in the regiment that came from camp Robinson have a little more schooling than high school.

There is a heavy mist in the air this morning. We are so close to the ocean I guess. I get a good view of the ocean several times a day.

Dad, I know you are wondering just what I will be doing. I can be and might be anything from a first aid man on the front lines to working in an evacuation hospital-wherever I am needed most. It is quite possible I may have a hundred different jobs before this war is over.

The regiment is supposed to be a crack outfit. Most of the fellows have been in the army 18 mos., having gone through two 'maneuvers.

They have had a lot of guard detail work. So the main rumor has it we are going to some island to do guard duty. Of course we may never leave the coast. I do know we are going somewhere and are just waiting until we are equipped and everything checked.

You may have read articles on the medics. We are supposed to be immune from gun fire, however in this war I doubt it very much. We all have white arm bands with the Geneva Red Cross on them.

In any group of men, there is always a medic detachment. I really am proud of the division I am representing in this army. Tell everyone hello.

With love,
George

"Didn't have a hard enough job? He was serving his country…during wartime! But he wasn't sure that was enough. He wanted to do more than they were asking of him. That was George. But it was countless other young men of that day as well."

"At the risk of sounding condescending, I'm going to say that the majority of people younger than 60 or 65 probably don't have a true appreciation of what it means to be an American. There was a certain pride and feelings of honor and integrity that came with serving our country that just doesn't seem to be there now. Or rather, it's the pride in our soldiers and respect for them that isn't what it should be these days."

"Our men and women serving today don't get near the respect they deserve; respect for being protectors of our freedom and constitution. To many, it's merely the job or profession they chose."

"I know that sounds a bit judgmental, but unless you lived through the depression and/or WWII, I don't think you have experienced true American spirit; being thankful for what you had — however little it was and giving unselfishly of yourself to protect the rights and freedoms of this country and other countries that had been devastated by the evil of Hitler and the Japanese."

"There was never any question about the need to be involved. And when the Japanese attacked Pearl Harbor, the unity and determination of the American people *and* our allies was such that I doubt it will ever be equaled."

"The attack on our country on September 11, 2001, has been compared to the attack on our nation on Dec. 7, 1941, but truthfully, there is very little comparison to be made. Yes, they were both brutal attacks on our nation's soil and yes, many innocent lives were lost as a result of both tragic events. But that's where the similarities end."

"I know there was an outpouring of generosity and support reaching from across the country to help those in need and in pain and I know as Americans we were shocked and angered that someone would dare to do something of this magnitude to the United States of America! But it took only days, if not hours, for many of these same citizens to get over it."

"You think I'm wrong? Then why were we so torn in our opinions on fighting back? Why are we, as a nation, divided against each other instead of being united against our enemies regarding guarding our nation against terrorism?"

"And why did we understand the importance of taking a no-tolerance attitude toward Nazi-ism, the Japanese hunger for power and communism then but are so quick to defend the rights of a culture which clearly states that we (infidels) should be destroyed?"

"You don't believe me? Then why are political correctness and religious tolerance such a big deal? Times are tough in America today in many ways like they were tough back then. But American spirit isn't the same — the strength and pride of being an American is severely lacking."

"If you don't agree, ask yourself what kind of world would we be living in today if we would have given as much care to be politically correct toward the Nazis as we are with Islam? There was no doubt in anyone's mind that Hitler had to be stopped. 'Just' because the millions of people being annihilated were half a world away didn't mean it wasn't our problem. What kind of human beings would we have been if we would have had the mind set of 'that's there-not here, so why should I worry about it', or 'let them fight their own war', or 'why should someone I love die for someone I don't even know?'? Sound familiar?"

"I know some people-maybe even a lot of people-would say I'm prejudiced or racist. But that's okay. They have a right to feel that way just like I have a right to feel the way I do. What those people need to know, however, is that the only reason they have the freedom to feel the way they do is because of people who weren't afraid to say 'no' to tolerance and political correctness."

"Those of us who *do* remember what it was to be an American over half a century ago watch the news and shake our head in disbelief."

"In some ways we've made tremendous progress over the years, but in many key areas we've lost precious and crucial values; values that George and Charles and nearly three hundred thousand others died for."

"I was never made to feel that my big brother died for nothing and it is shameful for anyone to make our military families feel that way now."

"I don't have any idea why or how George ended up as a medic. I guess I really didn't think about it then and years later when I did, there was no one left to ask. But when he wrote this letter he knew there was no such thing as being immune from gunfire in war."

"Medics were 'marked' with white arm bands that had the traditional Red Cross on them and carried medical supply bags over their shoulder. Their primary function was to administer first aid to the wounded and start them toward the rear of the line to safety."

"Medics would control bleeding, immobilize broken limbs, apply bandages, administer sulfa powder and tablets, morphine and plasma and assess the severity of a man's condition."

"The sulfa powder and tablets were military staples for soldiers as well as medics-most likely saving countless lives. Each soldier had a small pouch attached to his belt that contained sulfa pills and powder and bandages. In case of injury they were to immediately swallow the pills and pour the powder on the opened wound to cut the risk of infection."

"The problem was that oftentimes the guys left their belts in their foxholes to make moving along the ground and heavy brush easier. This made it even more crucial for medics to keep an ample supply with them."

"Medics were also armed and fully trained to fight and did so more often than not. But when push came to shove, their number one priority was to tend to the wounded."

"There were times when it worked liked it was supposed to, but war isn't a game and the Japanese had never heard of 'fighting fair'. As a matter of fact, they specifically targeted the medics. Their reasoning; getting rid of the medics would leave nobody to take care of the wounded-resulting in a higher number of casualties."

"Shortly after George died we received a letter from his commanding officer. It was the duty of the commanding officer to write a letter to each and every parent and wife who lost a loved one. But it was comforting just the same. To read words of praise and admiration for George-words of appreciation for his life and the loss of it-helped…a little. George said he was proud of what he was doing in the effort to win the war and we were proud of him, too. I always will always be proud of George for what he did and for who he was."

April 5, 1945

(letter from Commanding Officer of the 103rd Infantry
Regiment)

Dear Mr. Burks

*As Commanding Officer of the 103rd Infantry Regiment of which
your son, George, was a member, I wish to extend my personal
condolences at your loss. He was killed in action on 23 March 1945
while recapturing from the Japanese forces, Luzon Island which was
lost to us when they attacked without warning some three years ago.*

*He was buried in the United States Armed Forces Cemetery,
Manila Number 1, Luzon, with a burial service benefitting his faith.
George was an excellent soldier, well-liked by all officers and enlisted
men. He gave his life valiantly for a cause we know to be righteous
and which cannot fail.*

*Many men like him will carry on until the enemy is destroyed and
the democratic way of life, cherished by all of us, shall again prevail
throughout the world. The loss of your son is deeply felt by myself
and his fellow soldiers. His bravery and the cause for which he gave
his life will forever be a monument to his memory.*

Sincerely yours,
Joseph P. Cleland
Colonel, Infantry

Dec. 5ᵗʰ, 1942

Dearest Dad,

I received your letter yesterday that was written Thursday night of Oct. 15ᵗʰ. Also received Inah's card mailed November 17.

I was glad to hear Helen had heard from Charles that he was in Australia, because his chances are very good that he will never leave there.

What branch or outfit did Gareth get in? Wynette seems to think he will get limited service. I hope you took your sick leave while he was home. Did you go see Harold? I guess Harold is home by now, and I hope so. What are his plans? Does he think he will go to the army?

We now have a canteen in camp. We can buy just about anything we need, however I am out of stationary, so if you could send some it would be appreciated very much. Also some airmail stamps. We also have a show once a week in camp now. I have seen two shows, "Here Comes the Fleet" and "My Favorite Spy".

Benny have you been writing my any letters? I wish you would write and tell me a lot of the town news.

I had turkey for Thanksgiving. The way the weather is here, it doesn't seem possible that it is only 3 weeks until Christmas.

I went swimming yesterday afternoon. The water was quite cool, as the pool is formed by a spring.

Our mail service should be pretty good now so please write quite often. I have been a little lax in writing the past 10 days but promise to write every few days.

With love,

George

P.S. Merry Christmas and a Happy New Year

"I don't know for certain what George meant, but I think he was saying that Charles would most likely be in Australia until he was sent home. And since Australia was pretty safe at that point, being there was good news. Charles had been in Papua New Guinea where the fighting was going on at that time, so at least he was out of that. But this could have been around the time Charles first got sick with Malaria. I'm honestly not sure. What I do know is that about six months later Charles died."

"George definitely didn't know it at the time, but his words were all too true; Charles never did leave to come home. Not the way we wanted him to, anyway. They say time heals all wounds. And it does. But no matter how much time passes, there is always at least a hint of a scar. I know that's true because to stop and think about those days even now makes me sad…makes me wish that things would have been very different for me and my family."

"If nothing else is derived from George's desire to have us send stationery and stamps, I hope people take to heart the need of a soldier to feel connected to the ones he loves back home and the responsibility of those loved ones to make sure that connection is strong and constant. Internet, cell phone, letters; it doesn't matter how, it just matters that you do."

"But why? Why is that connection so important when a soldier obviously has plenty to keep them busy-especially during wartime?"

"For George, the question of why is easy. George wanted to hear from us and wanted all the news from home because he genuinely cared about the people he loved."

"I know it's only normal to put a deceased loved one on a pedestal, but George really didn't have any personal enemies. He didn't have a mean bone in his body. He was caring and compassionate and really did think of others before himself."

"And as far as letting people know he loved them, I'm sure George died with little or no regrets on that one. I know how much he loved me, and I feel sure he knew how much I loved him. For being just a kid at the time, I did a decent job of keeping in touch."

"It's only natural to have a few regrets, though; things like not writing more or saying more than the normal 'I love you'. But families didn't dwell on the fact that their loved ones might not come home."

"We knew it was a possibility. Every time there was a new casualties list printed you got that kick-in-the-gut reminder that it was possible. So we took every opportunity we got to George know how much we loved him, but we didn't think about why we took those opportunities. We couldn't. Instead, we just kept hoping and praying for his safe return home.

That's what everyone did. And for some those prayers were answered the way they wanted them to be. For others like us, they were just answered."

February 8, 1943

Dearest Harold,

I received your letter written on the 7th of January yesterday. I have some spare time this morning so will answer it. My gun is dirty, so I must clean it too.

No, I was not so surprised to hear from you and I had a letter from Helen written on the 15th of January which had been written in Crocker. I received her letter 9 days ago.

There is one thing I would like to see you do next fall, and that is to go on to school even if to no place but Iberia Junior college. Of course, there has to be a desire before anything can be gained.

Don't be in any rush for the army-wait as long as you can because this war's end is not far off. If you don't want more school, then marry that girl. Who is she?

Be sure and send me all the Crocker gossip-telling me the latest drug store rumors. I do know that town is quite a place, but we get out of anything just what we put in it.

Your letter sounded so much like the Harold I would like to see so much, and I do hope that you continue in the frame of mind you are now in.

Dad, the watch finally met disaster. The crystal is broken. As long as I had that watch on my wrist, and as many places as it has gone, it had to get broken in my barracks bag. I intended to buy the watch from you because fifty years from now I can tell all my grandchildren all that happened to it.

How is Jack Dawson getting along? I've had reasons to think about him the past week.

Tell all hello and that I am enjoying myself as much as possible. No, really it isn't or hasn't been too bad. I was glad Helen had a nice visit with you all.

Benny, every once in a while, while climbing these mountains, I think of how you used to like to climb the 'ant hill' from the spring. If you were with me, you could get all the climbing you wanted. How are the dogs? School? It has been quite a while since I've heard from you.

With love,
George

"Harold James was my brother-he was next to the youngest after me. George worried so much about Harold, but he had reasons to. Harold had been in some trouble-nothing that would be considered serious these days, but Dad and Mom decided they did not want it to get any worse, so they did what they thought best; they sent to a reform school for a brief time."

"George knew this, and knew Harold was home, and that that part of his life was behind him. He wanted Harold to realize what a great guy he was, and live up to his potential. I think this will all make even more sense if I explain a few things about our family."

"My brothers and sisters were actually my half-siblings (I use the word 'were' because I am the only one still living). Their mother died giving birth to Harold; leaving Dad with six children ranging from a newborn to thirteen."

"He was at a loss as to how he would be able to care for a newborn and provide for his familly. Anyone would be, but for a man back then, it was next to unthinkable. Dad certainly didn't want or expect my two oldest sisters, Helen and Wynette to become instant mothers. They were still children themselves; children dealing with the loss of their mother."

"So, in his grief and at the prodding of well-meaning friends, Dad made a decision he regretted for the rest of his life. He allowed a family by the name of Guffy to take Harold into their home to care for him until he was more capable of doing so."

"As it turns out his regrets were well-founded. The family that took him only did it for the little bit of money Dad gave them to help provide for Harold. Those first few years of Harold's life were anything but loving and nurturing. Mr. and Mrs. Guffy were harsh and even abusive at times."

"Dad spent as much time as he possibly could with Harold during that time but never suspected a thing. The people he saw were not the people Harold lived with, so to speak. And Harold was too small to know to say anything. He didn't really know any better."

"He knew the time spent with Dad and the rest of the kids was different, but he was just too little to know how or what to say. The time away from Dad and our brothers and sisters left scars on Harold for many, many years and Dad never fully got over the guilt he felt because of it. He felt like he should have seen what was happening. He felt like the troubles Harold had later on were his fault."

"Six years after his wife, Rosa, died, Dad met and married Mom. By then Helen was nineteen and married to Charles. Wynette, Gareth, Gertrude, George, and Harold were seventeen, fifteen, thirteen, eight and six. Talk about instant family! But that didn't matter to Mom. Even though she was thirty-four and had not been married prior to marrying Dad, she came from a large family herself, *and* had been teaching school for several years."

"She was great with the kids and she loved them all as if they were her biological children. It wasn't always easy, though — especially for the girls. More specifically, it was most difficult for Wynette."

"Adjusting to a new mother as a teenager after so many years of helping run their household with Helen, Wynette couldn't (or wouldn't) let Mom into her heart for the first year or two. Gertrude's big adjustment was that she had to learn she didn't have to feel guilty about being happy. She also had to learn that she wasn't betraying her mother or her older sister by being happy."

"Even though Gareth was a teenager too, he said it was a very easy adjustment for him. His memories of his mother were vague, and Mom worked hard to make them feel loved and to give them the sense of family that had been missing without the presence of a mother in the house for so long."

"He told me years later when we were talking about the whole situation, how much he loved Mom, and that he had a tremendous amount of respect for her. He said he knew it couldn't have been easy, but that she did her best to make a loving, happy home for them all. George and Harold had no memories of their birth mother, so Mom was the only mother George and Harold ever really had. Harold was more than willing to accept Mom as his own even though he sometimes struggled. It wasn't always easy for Harold to know how to give and receive love."

"Mom loved each and every one of us kids, but I think it would be fair to say that she had a special place in her heart for Harold. Having lived with an abusive father, herself, she knew what it was like for him. She knew how important it was to make him feel safe and loved." As for me…I was born about a year after Dad and Mom got married-bringing the total in our family to eight (plus Helen and Charles)."

"When all was said and done, our family wasn't much different from most other families of the day. We loved, laughed, worked hard, argued, worshipped, celebrated, grieved, and went about the business of living life. And like so many other families in the 40s, we sacrificed one of our own for the greatest nation on earth.

"But back to George's letter…Harold did go into the army, he went to Jr. College, and he married the girl — Irene. George knew Harold joined the army, went to Iberia Jr. College and that Harold and Irene planned to marry. But what he didn't know was that Harold lived a long, happy, honorable, and productive life. He made a good living, and enjoyed almost fifty years of marriage to Irene before she died. They were unable to have children, but he was a wonderful and loving uncle. He loved to joke around with the kids and let them know how much he cared."

"Even though Harold was seven years older than me and George was ten years older, the three of us were really close. But after George's death, Harold and I became even closer; a relationship we enjoyed until his death on March 23, 2007, which was sixty-two years to the day that George was killed. Somehow I don't think that was a coincidence."

"There are a lot of things I wish George would have lived to see and do. But seeing the man Harold became is definitely at the top of the list. Then again, I like to believe that somehow George does know that Harold was a good man and a wonderful brother."

"Dad gave George his watch that day we put him on the train in Jefferson City. I also remember George being really proud of having it. I know by today's standards a watch doesn't seem all that important, but a man's watch was important to him back then. It was a valuable possession- something he took pride in owning."

"In a way it symbolized your being a man. Besides, you have to remember that the depression hadn't been over very long, and like most people, Dad and Mom were still trying to get back on their feet. Having something of value to give George was important to Dad.

"You can be sure that George hadn't missed the message in Dad's gesture. Had he lived to marry and have a family, I have no doubt he would have done just what he planned to do; tell story after story of his service to our country and of the many places he and the watch traveled. Having that watch was George's something to hang on to-his hope that he would have a future after the war. Our boys had to believe they had a future-it's what gave them the will to go on in spite of the pure hell they were in. Sadly, for George and thousands of others, hoping was as far as it went. That's just another reason I want to tell George's story."

"I don't know why he didn't just come right out and say it, but I think George's mention of Jack was his way of saying he had a toothache or needed something in the way of dental work. I can't think of any other reason why George would have said he'd needed to think of him."

"Jack was Dad's first cousin, and a dentist. He was also a brother to Geraldine, the teacher who had asked about the funeral when George died. Jack spent a lot of time at our house and we thought the world of him."

"It's funny how reading simple little things like that bring back so many memories. I hadn't thought of Jack in years."

"The 'ant hill' was a steep hill we went down to get to a spring right by our house. We loved that place and spent a lot of time there. In spite of the fact that they were older than me, George and Harold were really great about letting me tag along with them-especially when they were playing on the 'ant hill'."

"I remember one time I fell in and Harold had to pull me out so I wouldn't drown. I was pretty young and hadn't learned to swim all that well yet. Good thing he was there."

We'd catch crawdads there, too. And in the winter I can remember sliding down it when there was snow on the ground; racing to see who could get to the bottom first without falling and then racing back up. I guess every kid has someplace special like that-a place that makes them feel adventurous or bigger than life. The 'ant hill' was that for me — partly because George and Harold were there to watch out for me and take all my adventures with me."

March 26, 1943

Dear Dad,

   Been quite a while since I've had a letter from you, so I find the topics for a letter scarce. The weather-it's been quite a while since it has rained very long but it showers here every few days. Almost always there is a nice saltwater breeze, but the sun gets quite hot at times. I am still in best of health, getting along just swell.

   Happy birthday, Harold! Harold, how about a few lines telling me about yourself?

   I have been looking for my package any day now, as Wynette has answered a letter that I wrote February 10th. It is just about this time of year that everything begins to denote spring. Tell everyone hello, and that although I don't write to some of them, I do think of them quite often.

All my love,
George

"At this point, George was in the Solomon Islands. The saltwater breeze he was referring to was coming from the Guadalcanal. For obvious security reasons George was not often permitted to tell us where he was. If he would have, the censorship department would have cut those sections out of the letter before allowing it to be sent to us."

"They did that, you know. The letters a soldier wrote home were read by a censor to ensure troop movements, locations and other information wasn't being divulged. Most soldiers knew what they could and couldn't say, so it was usually not an issue, but once in a while they would find something unacceptable and cut it out. After reading the letters they would stamp them with a censorship stamp, tape the envelope shut and send it on its way to the states."

"George's letters were usually more about how he was rather than where he was or what he was doing. But as you'll see later on there was a point when he was able to give us a brief 'road map' as to where he had been."

"Not knowing was frustrating to families-especially families like ours who couldn't even find some of the places on a globe the newspapers and newsreels said American troops were fighting in."

"But I will have to say that the media worked hard to provide the American public with information as to what was going on during the war and where it was going on at."

"Was there sensationalism? Yes, but very little. The media was a lot more respectful and professional back then than they are now. Were there graphic pictures, newsreels, and reports? Yes. But it was all done for such different reasons than it is today. The newsreels, reports, and articles were a family's link to their loved one and a means to keep the war effort foremost in the minds of people here at home. Rationing and shortages of gas, wool, rubber, sugar, and a lot of other things weren't easy. These news reels reminded us of our patriotic duty. They were a salute to our military's efforts to preserve our freedom and the freedom of our fellow man overseas. Today the sensationalism seems to be for shock value."

"I know I've said this more than once, but it's really important to me that anyone who reads this knows just how thoughtful and unselfish George was. In a strange sort of way, the fact that George died doing his job-taking care of the wounded-makes sense. He was just being George-thinking of others before himself."

March 28, 1943

Dear Dad,

I had three letters today one from you dated Feb. 23 and the other two were from Helen and Harold.

So glad the package is on the way. I was afraid maybe you hadn't received my slip, so I got another which I sent to Helen. Was afraid the col. might remember you name on the previous slip. I told Helen if she couldn't find a good knife to send you the slip. I have seen knives that sold for $2 at home bring $15 here. The package will be appreciated more than I can ever thank you. I also know how hard it is to buy that stuff at home.

Our food is good enough, and we get plenty of it, but the variety never changes much. I'd give a month's pay to sit down to a table full of milk, fresh eggs, hot rolls, and butter.

Harold, I did enjoy your letter of February 19*th*. Looks like you are set on the army. Hope you like it and do try to get all you can from it. Everything must be changed around Crocker quite a lot now.

Everything is as usual here. Coconuts are still great. About 11 crops a year are grown here.

We have a nice shower made from the tent, and I intend to use it in a few minutes then take a nap.

I too, am as usual. In best of health, and not working too hard.

Please tell everyone hello. Walter still working at the Fort, I guess?

So glad Gareth is liking the army so well.

From now on each place we land is apt to be worse. Never worry about me-still hoping for that Christmas dream.

All my love,
George

"Knives, watches, jewelry and other similar items were hot items with the natives. The guys were always asking folks back home to send these things for them to trade to the natives for souvenirs and laundry services. Most of them had knives and watches they'd brought with them, but just like the watch Dad gave George the day we put him on the train, they were precious reminders of family and home, and not up for trade. Instead, we'd send the cheapest ones we could find so they could do their trading."

"George loved to eat as much or more than I do. Having the fresh coconuts and other tropical fruits was undoubtedly a lifesaver from field rations. But there really is no place like home and a meal cooked by Mom; especially her rolls and the milk, cream and butter we had from our milk cow."

"Censorship kept George from saying much more. I know that had to be frustrating to Dad and Mom, but maybe it was better that they didn't know. I remember asking things like, 'Do you think George was there?' when we would hear about something that happened. Charles was still alive when this letter was written, so I didn't realize yet just how much a part of war dying was. At this point I was still like most boys my age. I believed that our troops could go in and save the day and that the only ones who got hurt were the bad guys."

"Knowing what I know now about what went on over there makes me sad for George…for all those boys. They were so brave, but I know they had to be scared. The fact that George even mentioned it tells me he was at least a little apprehensive."

"Most of the young men there were no different than George; just good kids from small towns or fresh off the farm. They were young men who loved their country and wanted to do their part to stop Hitler and the Japanese. They were kids who knew what it was to be honorable. They knew right from wrong and wanted to help make things right in the world once again."

"Don't worry? Not likely. I knew Mom and Dad worried about George but looking at it now from a parent's point of view, I can only imagine how hard it was for them. I know they were concerned for Charles, too."

"Later, Gareth and Harold both went to Europe and saw action over there. So when it came to worrying, Dad and Mom had more than their fair share of practice. My sister Wynette's husband, Rob, was also in the army during the war, but never left the country.

"While I doubt I thought much about it at the time, it is interesting now to notice that George is talking about a Christmas dream in a letter he wrote in March. There was a war going on and tours of duty or deployments as they're called now didn't really exist. Your tour of duty was as long as it needed to be. In most cases, that meant you were there for the duration of conflict wherever you were at."

"In some of George's letters that follow, he will make other references to being home for Christmas. Maybe there was some talk about them going home by then. History would seem to say otherwise since the most decisive battles in the South Pacific didn't occur until late in the war, but it really doesn't matter. I'm sure knowing they were there for the duration didn't keep any soldier from hoping for the day they got to go home any more than it did George."

FYI

George E. Burks was a member of Company E in the 103rd Infantry Regiment, 43rd Infantry Division. When he got on the train that day in Jefferson City, MO, he went to Camp Robison, Arkansas for basic training before going on to Camp Ord, California. After he arrived in California, his family had no idea how long it would be before he shipped out, where he would go, or even what his duties would be. They just knew he would soon be a bona fide soldier in a bona fide war.

Shortly after George arrived in Ft. Ord, California, he, and the rest of the 103rd (his regiment) set sail for the South Pacific. They arrived in New Zealand in October of 1942 to prepare for battle in various campaigns throughout the South Pacific. Censorship prevented our men from coming right out and telling their families where they were, but if they were astute enough, they thought of ways to let them know. For instance: in one letter, George (for no particular reason) wrote that he had been thinking of a family back home-especially their son, Russell. This may not seem like much, but this one little 'clue' told my family that at the time he was writing that particular letter, he was in the Russell Islands.

Families listened intently to their radios each evening and devoured newspaper articles from the correspondents overseas for information on the war's progress. Censorship kept them from knowing exactly where their loved ones were, but they paid attention to where the fighting was taking place. Then after censorship restrictions were loosened up a bit, George and soldiers just like him were able to tell their families where they had been (not where they were going). Once they knew where he had been, they would have known what kind of action he had seen.

August 5, 1943

Dearest Dad,

I have been receiving yours and Benny's letters the past two weeks quite regularly but haven't had much time to answer them.

It has been raining this morning, but now looks as if the sun is trying to come out now. The heat has been quite bad here.

Benny, I have enjoyed your letters so much. Congratulations upon your great success on selling so many papers.

Glad to hear Inah is getting along so swell and do hope she continues on the road to better health.

Have lost a few lbs. of weight, but it hasn't hurt me any. Am sleeping great, and our food is good even though the hours of eating are irregular.

This is the first letter I have written in over three weeks. I am hoping that you have heard from me indirectly during that period of time, as I tried three ways to get messages to you.

All my love,
George

"The way this letter sounds, you'd think George was writing from college or something. The day he wrote this letter, though, was the first day George was involved in serious combat. August 5th, 1943 was the day the United States claimed victory at Munda airfield."

"By the time we had gotten this letter I'm sure we had heard about the battle, but I'm just as sure we had no idea George had been a part of it. As I've said before, that information wouldn't come until later on when he could fill in the details of where he'd been."

"Something else we would learn about that day is that George received a commendation for a Distinguished Service Cross because of his heroism during the battle for Munda airfield."

"This is one of the shortest letters George wrote, but looking at it now, I think he wrote it to remind himself there was a world out there that wasn't as ugly as the one he'd been a part of that day. Up to this point George had been pretty descriptive of the work he did. What he didn't say when he wrote this letter on the evening of August 5th, 1943 said just as much or more."

"We were also still reeling from the news of Charles' death a few weeks earlier. The fact that George and Charles were so close may make some people think George would have been distracted that day because of his grief."

"Not George. He was definitely still grieving, but George wasn't the type of man to put others in danger because he wasn't doing his job to the best of his ability."

"Instead, George went above and beyond the call of duty. The DSC commendation proves that. And I know in my heart that to some extent his actions were meant to honor Charles."

"I'd almost forgotten about selling papers. There was a husband and wife (I can't remember their names) who drove a panel van. They'd pick me and a few other boys up in the afternoons to take us over to Ft. Wood (Fort Leonard Wood army base) where we'd sell newspapers door to door."

"We each had our own routes on the base. I was lucky enough to have officer's quarters on mine, so I did pretty well. I don't remember how much we made, but I remember it being enough to go to the movies on and other things like that."

"I only did it in the summer. Mom and Dad didn't want me doing it after school. Homework and chores were more important."

"Inah Burks was our cousin. Her father, Uncle Howard and Dad were brothers. She was what people called and 'old maid'-meaning she never married. She lived her whole life with Uncle Howard and Aunt Nancy except the last three years which she had to spend in Mt. Vernon* to be treated for tuberculosis."

"Inah was a sweet person and everyone loved her. She taught Sunday School at our church until she got sick. She was just one of those people that had a kind word and a smile for everyone. I don't know why she never married. Any guy would have been lucky to have her."

"Inah was George's favorite cousin. A lot of George's letters have been lost through the years, but I can tell you that very few of them did not include something about Inah. He wanted to make sure we kept him up to date on her condition. He knew she would never say anything in her letters to him that might make him worry. I know this may sound strange, but when Inah died I remember thinking it was a relief that George did not have to know about it. But I also remember worrying that George's death would make Inah's TB worse. Inah was only thirty-nine when she died — another life cut way too short. I've had to deal with a lot of those."

"George had been engaged in fierce battle-during the 'last three weeks' he hadn't written. By the time we received this letter Dad and Mom probably had no trouble putting two-and-two together. As for the three ways he'd tried to get messages to us? I have no idea what they were or if he was successful. Mom and Dad didn't say. It wasn't unusual, though, for guys to try to get word back home in any number of ways."

"One way soldiers got word to people back home was through fellow soldiers lucky enough to get sent back home. These guys would call or come see their buddy's family. They'd bring mementos, stories, and words of from assurance. Unless they were wounded or had somehow lucked out, not too many guys came home 'just because' between 1941 and 1946, so while it did happen, no visiting soldier ever came to our door."

"Another possibility, even though it was a slim one, was the newsreel. Going to the movie theater was our main source of entertainment back in those days. Americans went to the movies (usually on the weekend) as eager for the newsreels about the war as they were to see Errol Flynn, John Wayne and Jimmy Stewart bombing Tokyo, sinking German warships and sending the Nazis high-tailing it back to their foxholes."

"The AP (Associated Press) was right in the thick of it- they went just about anywhere and everywhere the troops did. These newsreels showed our boys fighting from the air, on the ground and in the water. They showed victory, defeat, living conditions, camaraderie, injured soldiers, and even death (from a distance). Watching the newsreels in the off chance you would catch a glimpse of a son, husband, brother, or sweetheart wasn't something we took lightly. Soldiers being filmed in non-combat situations were just as eager to 'say' hi to everyone back home by waving and smiling for the camera. You just always hoped one of them would be your family member. I don't remember Mom and Dad going to the movies, but my buddies and I did, thanks to the money we earned from our paper routs. Helen and the rest of my brothers and sisters did, too, but unfortunately we never saw George on any of those reels."

FYI

* In September of 1907, the Missouri State Sanatorium opened in Mt. Vernon, MO for the sole purpose of treating tuberculosis. Tuberculosis is a highly infectious disease caused by bacterium that has been around for centuries. While it usually affects the lungs, it can involve almost any organ in the body. During the 1930s and 40s, TB reached epidemic proportions and was the leading cause of death in the United States. When someone got TB, they were sent to a sanatorium such as Mt. Vernon to be treated (usually 12-24 months) to avoid infecting others. Until the mid-1940's, there was no cure, and many people died from it. But in the mid 40's it was discovered that strong antibiotics could cure tuberculosis.

The state sanatorium in Mt. Vernon, MO is still in operation today. But today its emphasis is on cardiac procedures and therapy and treatment for patients with paralysis. Thankfully, TB isn't the problem it once was.

Aug. 24, 1943

Dearest Dad,

Haven't been doing much this morning. Straightening the tent up and spent an hour checking my medical supplies. Yesterday, I worked pretty hard making tables for the tent. Been playing a few games of Pinochle each day, too.

Am almost over my cold and am feeling pretty good-now that my stomach can hold food. Believe I have gained a couple of lbs. this past two weeks.

Mail must be in today or tomorrow as we have had none for two weeks. They gave us our mail while we were on the front line, though, so I am not complaining.

Am waiting for my packages to be paid before I send you the three watches I have. The field glasses are to be given to Benny but are subject to recall.

It is a beautiful day. Sun is shining, yet a nice breeze keeps it from getting too hot. I have had a few thermometers broken by the heat here, and they register to 108! I would say the average temperature here is over 100.

We have fresh beef for dinner. Some of the fellows went hunting yesterday afternoon.

I know this beef won't taste like the nice steaks I had in Auckland New Zealand. That was the first port I landed in overseas. New Zealand is really a beautiful country. Great country for farm products. Next to home, that is where I'd like to be today.

From Auckland, I went to New Caledonia. I won't say much about that place because everything I did say would be to condemn the place. The mosquitoes were bad, and our training there was worse. We did everything from wading swamps to climbing mountains. Censoring regulations prevent me from going farther. However, Wynette can finish the trip to where I am now.

Benny, write and tell me about yourself. What are you doing?

Oh, yes! I hope you and Gareth had a nice visit together.

All my love,
George

Continued from above...

The censoring regulations were changed this afternoon, so I shall write more.

From New Caledonia, I went to Guadalcanal. Time spent there was short, and from there, Banika of the Russell Island group was next. I can mention no dates but believe you can fill in most of them.

From Banika on, the going was rough. We landed on Vangunu, where I first saw action. Rendova followed Vangunu, and from Rendova, to Manda (New Georgia Proper).

Packages were in the mail, but mine did not arrive. I know my packages were on Guadalcanal last Saturday, so I should get them sometime this week.

Will write again Friday if not before.

Mail must be in today or tomorrow as we have had none for two weeks. They gave us our mail while we were on the front line, though, so I am not complaining.

"Next to hearing that you were going home, hearing your name at 'mail call' was the next best thing. News from folks back home was a huge morale booster and the military knew how important that was to their overall success. But making sure the boys got mail on the front lines wasn't easy. Units were continually on the move, injury and death were constants and the injured were moved from place to place depending on the severity of their injuries. It wasn't unusual for a letter to make several stops before it actually got to where it was supposed to be. But when you think about it, it's a miracle any of the letters got through at all."

"As far as mail call went, though, I'm proud to say it was rare for George to not hear his name called. Between Dad and Mom, me, my brothers and sisters, other family members and friends, we kept George well supplied with mail to read and packages to open."

"I remember receiving the watches George mentions in this letter, but the field glasses never came. I sure wish they would have. It would have been nice to have something he especially wanted me to have. I'd have gladly given them back…to give them back would have meant George came back."

FYI

After training in Camp Robinson, Arkansas and Ft. Ord, California, George's unit sailed across the South Pacific to Auckland, New Zealand in October of 1942.

It is obvious from his letters that George fell in love with the beauty of this little country-the youngest country on earth. No doubt New Zealand's coastline, mountains and unique culture were something to behold-especially for a young man born and raised in a rural community and who had never traveled more than two or three hundred miles from home. I'm happy he and the other young men saw something beautiful before they were thrust into the horrors of the war. That was the very least they deserved.

From Auckland, George went to New Caledonia. New Caledonia, governed by France, was home to large American military installations during WWII. These bases were essential for combating Japan's advancement across the Pacific. Its location was advantageous for refueling and repairs for the allied forces, as well. But its dense jungle-like terrain and heavy, humid air was stifling; making the mosquitoes and the malaria they carried a major problem. From all indications, the three months spent in concentrated training there was more than enough for George.

Three months later they moved on to Guadalcanal in the Solomon Islands. Here they met little to no opposition; it was more of a training tool than anything. After spending a few days there, they met no resistance when they went in and occupied the Russell Islands (also in the Solomon's) in February of 1943.

Training. So much training-wasn't that what boot camp was for? Sure, but no amount of time in boot camp could have prepared our boys for the conditions they would face overseas. Having the opportunity to acclimate to the climate, jungle-like terrain and to learn the difference between good and bad wildlife, plants and food were crucial. But after spending four months there, the training stopped, and the real action began when they moved on in June of 1943...

The Vangunu and Rendova Islands in late June 1943, were George's first taste of all-out battle; minor resistance on the part of the Japanese, but nevertheless, real. So on August 5th, 1943, meeting strong and forceful resistance and suffering a large number of casualties, victory was ours. The much-needed airfield in Munda in the New Georgia Islands (also in the Solomon's) was wrestled away from the Japanese and was now in Allied possession; a crucial aspect of our success in the war."

Its takeover by the United States and our allies was one of the principal objectives of the campaign in the Solomon Islands. In other words, the training that George and the other soldiers had just completed was deliberate preparation for this day. As Americans, each of us can and should be extremely proud and thankful of the fact that they were (prepared).

George's 'roadmap' letter stops at Munda, which told his family that he was likely still at Munda waiting for the next move. Having this little 'road map' supplied the answer to the most often asked and most often unanswerable question families had during the war; 'where is he?'

For us, this letter should serve as a somber and humbling reminder of the integrity and selflessness of over sixteen million young Americans who fought fiercely and tirelessly for freedom.

October 31, 1943

Dear Dad,

Received your letter of October 17th yesterday. No doubt a great part of our mail is being flown from the states.

I see the camera, but unless you can send a few rolls of film, don't send a camera. Have you ever received any pictures from Helen that were sent to her? I have other pictures over here, but it would be impossible to send them. Shall have them after I come home. Do hope the pictures you took are ok. Seems like every letter I get from you, you have sent me another package. Suppose you realize the enjoyment we soldiers over here get from mail and packages from home. I have already written about sending my watch back.

Wrote Inah a few days ago. Glad to hear she is improving. Guess the rest of the town is about the same.

Maybe Harold getting married will be the best thing that has happened to him for some time.

Wynette wrote she had been sending a few of my letters on to you. I have probably written Wynette more letters than anyone else since I've been overseas. One reason is that I hear from her so often, but there have been some things on my mind I wanted to write about, yet hated to write them to you for fear you would worry over them.

I have a native made fish hook I shall send you before long. Intend to wait for a few other things-enough to make a small package. Please tell me when you receive your watches.

Took a trip the other day and was gone all day. The place where I got my watches has changed quite a lot. Haven't been doing much the past few days. Am now on a small outpost a short distance from the company. Really is a beautiful sight from here. We are on a small hill.

Benny, wish you were here to help me eat this large stalk of bananas hanging in front of me. Traded a native boy two bars of soap for them. The natives go for soap and pipes.

Watched a large lizard walk around for a while this afternoon. They look like small alligators.

I am feeling great.

All my love,
George

"We sent packages to George as often as we could. I remember sending him the school yearbook every year he was gone. I especially remember the year I put a picture of George in there."

"They were doing a tribute to former students serving in the war. The picture I put is one he'd sent home to us of him in swimming trunks. He got a big kick out of it. Mom didn't, though. She was embarrassed that I'd used a picture of him without a shirt on. We also sent things like chewing gum, stationery, the film for his camera he mentioned and stamps. The stationery and film were probably what he appreciated most. George was so good to write and send pictures of himself and his buddies."

"I was always excited when there were pictures with George's letters. I missed him a lot and seeing his face and seeing him smile was a really big deal to me. It was added proof that George was still George and that he was okay."

"Getting letters from George were just as important, though. The old adage that 'no news is good news'-wasn't true except if the news came in the form of a telegram-especially the hand-delivered kind."

"A lot of things have changed since the days of WWII. Some of them good-some of them not so good. One really good change is that today's military families have cell phones, web cams, Facebook, and email to help them stay in touch. When my grandson in-law was in Afghanistan, the webcam was a wonderful way for him and my granddaughter to see each other and talk. Trust me when I say that is definitely not something you should take that for granted."

Dec. 23, 1943

Dear Dad,

More mail tonight, but I didn't get any. Oh, yes, I did receive a letter from you a few days ago dated the 12th of December.

Very little to write about as usual. In the mess hall here, I have been listening to the radio while writing. The news is now on the air. Tonight I am thinking of where I was a year ago this night- on a tough problem in the hills of New Caledonia. Whatever you may be thinking, I assure you I am not expecting to see action again for some time. Please believe this, as you know I have yet to tell you a lie in my letters. There have been a few times that maybe I couldn't write all I wanted to.

Beer came in tonight. We will each get four bottles of Pabst apiece to last the month. One buddy here promised his, so on tomorrow night, I shall have 8.

Know all about Harold. Wrote him to tell you all if he hasn't already. As I mentioned in my last letter, please help him out of this jam.

Sorry to hear you have been sick with the flu. Hope it wasn't severe.

Should send some money home, but am saving it, thinking one of these days I will be where I can spend it.

Dad, I feel I should tell you that after the battle of Munda, I was written up for a DSC. I don't mean for you to spread this news. It is between you and me. I feel that the commendations I received were enough-all I deserved, as I was only doing my job like many others who weren't mentioned. The fact you mean so much to me is the only reason I write this now. Maybe sometime in the future I may receive the DSC or Silver Star.

Please never worry about me in any way. I do gamble-mainly because it is our past time amusement.

As for drinking, there is very, very little of that. Although, some get alcohol from the aid station.

Tell everyone hello.

With all my love,

George

"George was in Auckland, New Zealand when he wrote this letter-the same place they had docked when they first arrived in the South Pacific back in October of 1942."

"Following their victory at Munda and time spent fortifying the area the 43rd arrived back in New Zealand in December of 1943 for a period of rest and relaxation and to take on replacements."

"This period of rest was followed by several weeks of intense training in New Zealand to acclimate the replacement troops to the unit and to the conditions they would be facing. It was during this time in Auckland that George met Betty Edwards, the girl he fell in love with."

"George sent us several pictures of the two of them. This is the only letter I have that mentions her, but I remember several other letters he wrote that mentioned her; ones that indicated he planned to marry her."

"Dad and Mom corresponded with Betty's mother which also points to the fact that they were pretty serious. In her letters, Betty's mother was always genuinely complimentary of George."

"I know Dad and Mom appreciated these letters and were really proud to know George had not allowed what he had been through to harden his heart-that he was still the kind, loving, and honorable young man he was when we put him on that train."

"I think they it also gave them some peace of mind knowing that George had the joy of being in love in the last few years of his life."

"I wasn't really into girls at that age, so I'm sure I didn't think about how special that was at the time. But I do now and it's great to know that there was something (or someone) in George's life over there besides the war."

"Dad and Mom sent word to Betty and her mother that George had been killed. She probably knew something was wrong, though, because from what I remember George saying in his letters, he wrote Betty several times a week. When the letters stopped coming, I'm sure the possibility of George being gone had to cross her mind."

"I've often wondered what happened to Betty. Did she fall in love with someone else, get married and have a family? If so, did she tell her husband about the American she had been in love with?"

"Several years ago, I did a little searching on the internet for Betty Edwards in Auckland New Zealand. I knew that if she were still alive she would have been in her seventies, but with so little to go on, I didn't come up with anything. I'm not completely sure why I did it. Curiosity, I guess."

"Once they left Auckland, George went on to New Caledonia. New Caledonia served as the South Pacific headquarters for the American and Allied Forces' Navy and Army, as well as a repair station for our ships. New Caledonia wasn't a battlefield during WWII, but the Japanese tried unsuccessfully on several occasions to claim the island for their own in their attempt to take Australia and New Zealand."

"The tough situation George was talking about wasn't actual combat, but an intense training period which history tells us included random Japanese gun fire coming from their planes flying overhead. The jungle-type terrain and oppressive humidity and heat (that's really something, coming from a Missouri boy) were difficult to train in. It's no wonder George and the others were reflecting on how they had spent each Christmas since leaving home; reflecting and praying that by the next Christmas they would be at home."

"George's gentle assurance to Dad and Mom regarding his well-being is just what I would expect from him. That was just who George was. He was thoughtful and respectful of our folks. He knew the thought of losing another family member had to be weighing on their minds and he wanted to do whatever he could to help them not worry so much."

"Reading this almost makes me prouder of him than when I read about what he did in the war because it's just one more bit of 'evidence' of George's love for Mom and Dad. In the middle of a war it was important to him that Mom and Dad knew he still was the man they'd raised him to be. Mom and Dad raised us in a Christian home. Alcohol or gambling weren't even considered to be an option. George had always lived his faith fully. The fact that he was 'bragging' about having eight beers most likely upset Mom and Dad. But to George and many of the other soldiers, those occasional beers were nothing more than something besides stale, tepid water to drink. I'd say that's not asking too much considering the stress they lived under. And like he said, the gambling simply passed the time. They gambled with 'luxuries' like socks, those extra beers, stamps, food and trinkets sent from home. It was just a way to relieve the stress."

"George's reference to some getting alcohol from the aid station was his gentle, non-judgmental way of acknowledging the fact that for some, the war was more than they could take. But since giving up and going home wasn't an option, alcohol became a way of escape for those who couldn't deal with what was happening. It was their attempt at escape. If you were in that kind of shape, though, there was no way to escape. No amount of alcohol or anything else was going to erase the images embedded in their minds; images of seeing their buddies blown to bits or crying for their mothers as they lay dying. There was no escape from having to kill the enemy or be killed yourself. There was no escape from the fact that after each battle someone you usually shared a few laughs with someone who had shown you a picture of their sweetheart or kids yesterday would never be back."

"More than a few guys came back home damaged and broken for good. Guys I knew; my wife's cousin, for one. He and plenty of others were unable to escape the memories even though they came home safe; far away from where they had lived those nightmares. I guess that's something that couldn't be avoided. But it sure is a shame it has to happen."

"The DSC (Distinguished Service Cross) is the second highest award presented in the US Army; second only to the Medal of Honor. It is given to the soldier who 'displays extraordinary heroism during military action against an enemy of the United States'. These acts of heroism must have involved risk to his life so great that it set him apart from his comrades. To be written up for the DSC is not to be taken lightly. George was one of only forty people in the entire 43rd Division to receive one. Or to really put it into perspective, there were over sixteen million American soldiers in the military between the years of 1941 to 1946. During that time there was a total of 5,059 DSC awarded to soldiers of all branches of the military. That means less than one in every three hundred soldiers was awarded that honor. And George did. He earned that because of his bravery and dedication to America. George said he was just doing his job. But we all know it was a lot more than that…a whole lot more. And that makes me extremely proud."

March 9, 1944

Dearest Dad,

Have been receiving your letters quite regular, most of them are only two weeks old.

As you know by now, I am in civilization again. It is very beautiful here, and the people are very nice. Have been having a swell time-that is the reason I haven't written sooner and more often. Have a 3 and 5 day pass coming up this month.

You asked what division I was in. I had always thought you knew. It is the (censorship cut this out).

Oh yes, I don't expect to be home before Christmas, but I do feel I will be home by then.

Tried to go visit Charles grave, but found it impossible as his grave is in a separate field of action. Never expect to go there until after the war.

Very sorry I misunderstood your comments about my health. I've weighed 204 since I've been here, but I'm considerably harder than I was when I entered the service.

Had some pictures made — twelve to be exact. None seemed very good-they are in three different poses. Will send them all to you so you can have first choice. Don't expect them before 15 of April.

Still hear from Wynette and Helen quite often.

Guess Harold intends to make a go of his marriage. I wrote Helen to never let Harold have his insurance policy until he pays me all the premiums I have paid on it (all of them). I know he will never accumulate that much money.

Had a very nice letter from Inah. So glad to hear she is improving so much. As I have said before, it won't seem like Crocker to me unless she's home when I get there.

One of the fellows in company got a clipping from home saying the 103rd was coming home-it didn't say when, though. I know the first bunch will not leave until about the time of my birthday.

Am writing this in the Red Cross building here in camp. Radio is going and the ?? just came on. They sound swell to me.

Have you received any pictures of me lately? Got a big kick out of Benny putting that picture in the annual.

Please don't worry about me ever. I am forever dreaming of that day when I see you again.

Stopped drinking beer the first of the week and don't intend to start again while I am here. Will admit I drank a lot the first week. There were reasons for both of the above sentences.

In case you don't know where I am, feel sure Wynette does. Tell everyone hello.

All my love,
George

"Although the training in New Zealand was rigorous, for guys like George who had experienced the combat action they had, it probably seemed like a walk in the park. During the time off he had (the passes that he mentioned) he enjoyed spending time with Betty and even stayed at her mother's house. I wish George would have lived to know that he and I both fell in love with girls named Betty. He would have liked that. It sounds silly, I know, but George really appreciated little things like that."

"It hurts to read more of these comments about Harold. Yes, he did have a really rough time for a few years and yes, he caused Mom and Dad many a sleepless night. But he turned things around, and he did whatever he could to over the years to 'make it up' to Dad and Mom. He was a kind, hard-working man, a good husband and a wonderful brother and uncle. I was enormously proud of him for becoming the man he did. Don't get me wrong…George loved Harold. He just couldn't understand why Harold did some of the stuff he did. I guess none of us did. But then we weren't Harold. We didn't know what it was to feel as if you weren't wanted or loved. So who are we to say we wouldn't have done exactly the same things if we would have gone through what he did when he was little?"

"George could have saved the ink when he wrote telling Dad and Mom not to worry. That's just part of being a parent. George knew that, but I'm sure he felt it was his job to tell them not to."

"George's dream was our dream to; to welcome him home alive and well. Turns out that's all it was…a dream. Knowing that home was still where he wanted to be and that people like Inah were still in his heart makes me happy even to this day."

"It makes me happy to know he still felt like Crocker was home and let me tell you, if he would have made it back here, what a homecoming it would have been. Everyone in town would have been at that train station and we wouldn't have been able to leave until he had spoken to every single person there. That's just how it was with him."

"While I'm not certain of what George was trying to say here I am assuming it had something to do with trying to forget some things he had seen and done during combat."

"George wasn't a drinker. Like I said earlier, a beer now and then was just part of being over there but getting drunk was not something George would have done for the fun of it."

"I'm also sure he was not the only one who drank too much that 'first week'. When those boys stepped off that ship onto land that was friendly, safe, civilized and as much like home as anything they were going to get, it wasn't uncommon for them to whoop it up a bit too much. Mostly they were just trying to remind themselves that they were still normal-that who they were in combat wasn't who they would have to be forever. George's ability to see the foolishness and futility of his actions and quit…that was the man he really was."

March 27, 1944

Dearest Dad,

Have been receiving quite a few letters from you and Benny. Just haven't been in the mood to write lately.

Had a marvelous weekend. Met a very nice girl a couple of weeks ago and we spent most of Saturday together. Yesterday, I spent most all day at her house. Her mother is swell. Well, to make a long story short, it was the nicest day I've spent since coming into the army. The people are swell to us soldiers, and we all think the people here are grand. This is a great country. In a way, a great deal like the US, yet in many aspects, quite different.

Have my pictures now. They are not very good but am sending you a couple. Haven't used the film you sent yet but shall in the next two weeks.

Benny, you are pretty small to make a couple of 'cracks' you did in your letter. Always remember this: you are a little young to be delivering ultimatums. I do what I please as long as my conscience doesn't bother me, and so far it hasn't. Is that clear? Benny I have gambled with things far more important than a few dollars since I've been over here. Would it make any difference to gamble with money as well as with other things? When this war is over, things will be different. Until that time, I suppose I will have to know the reasons why. I'm not mad-just want you to get it all straight.

Had a five day pass last week and may get a three day one this week. Have started training lately, so I may not be able to get it.

The pipes are swell, Dad. I haven't smoked them much yet, though the big one will be a treasure I shall always hold on to. Thanks very much for the cigars, too. I shall treasure them and make them last for some time. Have been writing letters all morning, and it is now almost time for chow.

All my love,

George

"This is the only letter I have left which talks about Betty. I remember him dating a girl or two here at home, but never anyone serious. Even when he went to live with Helen and Charles to go to college he didn't date anyone in particular. The fact that he talks about her is why I think Betty was the real thing; a nice girl who genuinely cared for George the way he cared about her. George spent as much time as possible with her during his time in Auckland; much of it in her home where he got to know her mother, as well. I've already mentioned the fact that Mom felt comfortable writing to Betty's mother thanking her for their hospitality to George and that Betty's mom wrote back to Dad and Mom to tell them what a nice young man she thought George was, and that they could be proud of how he was conducting himself so far from home. It's obvious from the letter that she had taken the time to get to know him; just like any mother would get to know the young man her daughter loved. Mrs. Edwards' letter gives me the impression that she was giving her blessing to the relationship."

"I remember Mom reading more than one letter to Dad and me at the dinner table from Betty's mother, but for whatever reason, this is the only one I ended up with."

(Letter from Mrs. Edwards)

Dec 3, 1944

Dear Mr. and Mrs. Burks,

In answer to your welcome letter of appreciation, I might state that it was a pleasure to have and do for George while on leave in this country. He was always a gentleman in our company, and it reflects a great credit on you having such a good son. I took him among my friends, and he was always asked back to their homes. I do know George enjoyed his weekends and visits to my home, and he knows it was a pleasure for me to have him. I asked him to bring a friend on a three day leave and he brought along a very nice chap to share his room and a little home life, which is so good for these fellows. One would like to do something for those who are doing so much for them.

I had a letter from George yesterday from New Guinea. I do hope he stays there for a while longer. By the way, it is 5 months since he left New Zealand.

I was hoping he would get furlough back to America soon, but somehow it does not seem to be coming forth. He is in good spirits, and health, which is very helpful to one's moral.

I heard George is a wonderful soldier and is very much liked by the men of his company. I trust and pray that God spares him for you. I know the strain of having sons in battle is very hard on you, and may God grant you health and strength to shoulder your burden.

I wish you a beautiful new year.

Your sincere friend,
M. Edwards

But back to George's letter of March 27, 1944...

"I don't remember what I wrote to George, but in reading the letter, I'm going to guess it had something to do with his talking about the drinking and gambling. I was just thirteen at the time; things were still black and white to this little country boy. Where I come from people who drank and gambled were the rough, rowdy crowd that we wouldn't have had any association with. I'm sure I was just worried about him.

"Even when he got on to me, though, George made sure I knew he wasn't mad, and that when he got home he would be the same big brother I had loved and looked up to when he left. I'm glad he did because I feel bad even now for having hurt his feelings."

FYI

There is a time gap of five months between this letter and the next one. The gap covers the remaining time spent training and regrouping in New Zealand and the 43rd's arrival in New Guinea. References made to letters, packages, and pictures in the remaining letters that follow prove that. In less than a year, though, the letters would quit coming.

August 19, 1944

Dear Dad,

Just finished eating chow. Our meals are quite good now, lots of bread and plenty of coffee.

Haven't been receiving any mail lately. Don't' think any is coming in. Do hope my mail is going out.

Am feeling fine. Have lost a few pounds lately but could still lose more and never miss it.

I still haven't sent the camera,

Benny. Hope to have something else to send with it. Everything is quiet and safe around here-safer than the main street of Crocker.

In my spare time I play cribbage, go swimming in the surf at the beach close by.

Don't have your hopes too high on me being home by Christmas.

If I stay over here long enough, maybe when I do get home, I won't have to come back over here.

All my love,
George

"Telling them that he was safer where he was at than on Main Street in our little town of Crocker, MO had to be pretty reassuring to Mom and Dad since Crocker was as safe as any place could possibly be. The worse thing that happened around there was when the soldiers from nearby Ft. Leonard Wood got rowdy on weekend passes."

"Swimming in the ocean, playing cards, and fairly good food…sounds like the 43rd was enjoying a much-deserved break. For all the horrors they had already been through, the worst was yet to come, so I'm thankful George and his unit had this time."

"George made a few references to possibly being home within the year. Most of what he wrote about coming home was rumors he heard floating around…rumors most likely started by someone's wishful thinking. George said he was willing to bide his time if it meant his orders to go stateside meant he'd be home for good or that the war would be over, and everyone could come home. It had been over two years since we'd put George on the train, though, so we were as anxious to believe the rumors as he was. Each time a holiday came around we'd think, 'maybe by next year….'"

FYI

In July 1944, George's unit became part of the force that kept the Japanese from reinforcing their troops along the Drinimour River in New Guinea. Most of the action here had taken place earlier in the year but maintaining their position there would prove to be valuable for our invasion of the Philippine Islands a few months later. While they weren't as safe as they were in New Zealand, it was an easy assignment compared to their previous one.

The time in New Guinea he describes here is reminiscent of the hit musical, *South Pacific*. It takes place on an island in the South Pacific during WWII where the soldiers on the island enjoy the beauty of the island and its native people while protecting it from the Japanese. Knowing that at any moment things could change they give and take from each day what joy they can.

Dec 1, 1944 New Guinea

Dear Benny,

    Say, I have been looking for that school annual a long time. You remember you promised to mail it?

    I mailed you the camera a few days ago. You should receive it by the first of February.

    How are you getting along at school? What kind of ball team do we have this year? Shall be looking for a long letter giving all the gossip.

    Dad, I received your letter of the 14th, yesterday. Not much mail coming in lately, but I received quite a few letters last week.

    Am not sure that I wrote you that Mrs. E received your letter.

    It has been so long since I've been around Crocker. I am not sure if I know ??.

    Our chow has been quite good lately. Getting fresh meat often, plenty of bread, and fresh butter once in a while.

    I knew Benny would start to grow at about this age. I'll bet he still looks like a scarecrow. Has he learned to play checkers, yet?

    Sounds swell, all that gas. About summertime, we'll use it too.

    Am feeling great-better than usual since I've been here.

    Tell everyone hello.

All my love,

George

"George and the school annuals (yearbooks)-he loved them! He liked school and enjoyed knowing what was going on with kids he knew (mostly siblings of his friends) and with the basketball team."

"I remember how much fun it was to go watch him when he played on the basketball team when he was in high school. He was a starter and really good. His height definitely didn't go to waste. I don't know what happened to the annuals I sent him. I'm not sure what Dad and Mom received as far as his belongings after he died. I remember them being sent to the house, but his medals and a few other things are all I have left. I don't know what they did with the rest."

"As for the 'gossip' he wanted…I know I sound like a broken record, but George's interest in folks here at home was truly genuine. I hope my letters were all he hoped they would be."

"Believe it or not, there was a time I guess you could say I looked like a scare crow; thin and wiry."

"I was eleven when George left and nearly in the prime of my scare crow stage-something I don't think he ever experienced since he was tall and muscular-built just like Dad."

"Checkers…he only wished I couldn't play! Dad and I played checkers all the time and I was really good. George got a big kick out of watching us play. It's been a good while since I've played a game of checkers, but every game I ever played brought good memories of Dad and George."

FYI

Once again there is quite a gap in time between the letters we have. George wrote this during his final days in New Guinea before leaving for the Lingayen Gulf, Luzon (Philippine Islands). He, along with the rest of the 43rd would be part of the amphibious landing there in January 1945.

Japan knew all along that control of the islands of the South Pacific were crucial for their access to food and other materials. Their military tactics were ruthless in the effort to gain and/or keep control of the region. But for all their determination, that of the American and allied forces was greater. Battling against the Japanese was constant on some portions of the island until the infamous bombings of Hiroshima and Nagasaki in August of 1945, which for all practical purposes, ended World War ll.

December 17, 1944

Dear Dad,

Mail hasn't been coming in lately-letters I mean. Plenty of packages are arriving. Am enjoying that last pipe you sent, it is really a grand prize. Nothing new to write about, as usual. I do very little work, read a great deal when I can find something to read. Last night, I went out on a detail. I'm really feeling grand lately.

In his last letter, Harold was still complaining. He should know when he is well off. Wish I was in England. Am sure Gareth could write quite a few interesting stories.

Am wondering if Wynette is still in Crocker? Received a letter from Rob at his new camp. He sure got a grand break, and I am glad he did.

Saw a grand show two nights ago — "It Happened Tomorrow". It was quite different from the usual run of movies.

It has been raining the past few days. More rain that I had seen in a long time-even flooding our tents despite the deep ditches around them.

How is school, Benny? Maybe I'll get a letter from you shortly? I hope so.

Tell everyone hello.

All my love,
George

"George wrote this letter a week before Christmas and approximately two weeks before he left for what would be his final destination. I think the thing that stands out the most to me in this letter is family. We were on three different continents but still closely tied together. All three of my brothers-George, Gareth and Harold had the obvious bond of being active-duty servicemen. But it was more than that. It was the fact that our family didn't need geography to keep us close. We would have done just about anything to be able to be together, but the fact that we weren't didn't change how we felt. This closeness is something I'm thankful my brothers had to hold on to. I hope that somehow it made what they were doing a little less painful."

"Rob's 'grand break' George was talking about was the fact that Rob didn't have to go overseas. My brother in-law, Rob, was married to my sister, Wynette. I think the reason Rob was spared being sent overseas was the fact that he was older and a schoolteacher with excellent clerical skills. But for whatever reason, he ended up in a desk job somewhere in the states-something I think helped out a little bit as far as knowing what was going on.

"In one or two of George's earlier letters, he mentioned that Wynette probably knew where he was at."

"George admitted to telling Wynette things he didn't tell us. He did this so he wouldn't worry Dad and Mom and because he needed to be able to tell someone. And Wynette was a good person to tell those kinds of things to because she wasn't a touchy-feely kind of person. She would have read what George had to say, told him to keep a good head on his shoulders and come home safe."

"Losing her mom when she was just a little girl is what made her that way, I think, but she was also good to write George often and remind him that we all loved him and to be careful and stay strong."

"The other reason he mentioned Wynette knowing is that Rob had information a lot of other people wouldn't have had. No, I'm not saying Rob did anything illegal. I'm sure he didn't. I'm just as sure, though, that he kept his eyes and ears open for any information he could get about George's whereabouts, and then passed it on to Wynette as best he could."

"I also remember that Wynette came to stay with us in Crocker a good deal of the time Rob was gone. Wynette and Rob didn't have any children yet, so she decided to come back to Crocker to keep from being so lonely."

"It was pretty common for families to do this during the war. Households came together while the young men were off fighting. Combining ration stamps, finances, household and childcare responsibilities and being with someone who understood what you were going through helped make a stressful situation a bit easier."

"Wynette wasn't usually the easiest person to get along with, especially where Mom and Dad were concerned. It wasn't so much that she had anything against Mom personally. She just never fully accepted Dad marrying Mom after her mother died. But I don't recall her being unpleasant or hard to get along with. I actually remember Mom and Wynette getting along better than they ever did."

Feb. 18, 1945 Luzon

Dear Dad,

This is really a beautiful Sunday morning. I meant to go to church but got started at writing letters. I got everyone's mailed. Received a late letter dated January 9 letter from Harold. He seemed in good spirits and for once wasn't gripping about something. Benny's letter of December 31 arrived a few days ago.

Wynette wrote how much Benny has grown and Inah says he's really a handsome guy. His picture didn't look like I thought it would.

The snow and ice sounds great. On the line I went without a shirt as much as possible. It was hot and got almost as tan as the natives.

The one thing I've daydreamed a lot about is going out into the garden and picking some ripe tomatoes, some good cold milk, and fresh eggs. One afternoon we spent talking about good things to eat. We are eating from a kitchen now, but it isn't much better than the field rations we had.

Two days ago, we got our bags, and don't think we didn't enjoy a clean set of clothes. I never realized an army cot could be such a grand bed before, either. The ground gets hard and cold after so many nights. Yes, I really am feeling good. Best I've felt since New Zealand. Have lost only a few lbs. of weight, but about 4-6 inches from my waist.

The natives are doing most of the work pitching camp. Our clothes have already been done by the women. Can get a set of cottons washed for fifteen cents. Native labor is 50 cents a day. No need to write how anxious and glad they were to see us.

Our area is very nice here. A stream runs within 20 yards of this tent. There are large shade trees, too, and a grand breeze. The area is very clean, and I haven't seen a fly yet. We sure had plenty on the hill.

Rotation is still a laugh. Some fellows have been over here several months, I know. One officer in this company was at Buna and treated by Charles' outfit. Told me some interesting things.

We had three fellows leave for home in December, none in Jan., and one in February. Now that we are having a rest, the quota may be raised, but I doubt it. Please don't plan on my coming until I get there. I feel sure it will be before fall, though. Should get to see more of the island before long. Hope to write more of it then.
Tell everyone hello. Please don't worry. I'm as safe as being at home.

All my love,
George

"I don't know for sure what George was expecting me to look like. I did grow quite a bit in those two years-most every kid does. When he left I was a scrawny, awkward kid. I still wasn't very tall. I never did get as tall as George, Harold, Gareth and Dad. I was built more like Mom. That's okay though. I'm just proud that in spite of all that was going on around him, he cared about how much I was growing and changing. He didn't have to, but he did because that's what George did-he cared. But there was another reason that reaches deeper into the hearts and minds of a soldier. It's called familiarity."

"When a soldier left to go overseas during World War II they left to do a job and usually didn't return until they got it done. This means that it was not unusual for a soldier to be gone for three to four years (or more, in some cases). The military tried to 'limit' the time a soldier was overseas to no more than thirty-two months, but it didn't usually work out."

"Because they were away for so long (and under such horrendous circumstances) it was very important to them to know that when they came home they would be able to recognize it…go back to it. A solider wanted and needed to believe that things would be as he left them…even though he knew in his heart they wouldn't be."

"But the truth is that things wouldn't be the same because they couldn't be the same. Time marches on. Babies conceived before a soldier left were born, and were walking and talking by the time Dad came home. Sweethearts and wives sometimes didn't wait, breaking a soldier's heart. Wives had to step up and step into what had formerly been a man's world; giving them (women) confidence and skills they never knew they had."

"The soldier returning home brought with him more than he wanted to. The naïve, rambunctious boys who left thinking they were going to go over 'there' and whoop Hitler and his boys, or the 'Japs', returned as men who had lived through some of history's most gruesome events."

"They returned as men who had taken other men's lives many times over. They returned as men whose view of the world was calloused and realistic instead of naïve and simplistic. They returned as men whose hearts and minds longed and ached for the familiarity of life as it had been in days long gone."

"That's why a little brother's growth spurt, a baby sister's first date, or their own child's first day of school was so important to the men who had the future of the world in their hands."

"He sounds so casual. He makes it sound like being out on the line is as normal as milking the cow or delivering newspapers."

"Being on the line meant they were positioned for battle. There were times when our boys as well as other members of the Allied Forces arrived for the purpose of doing battle (Normandy and Munda, for instance). Many times, though, they arrived positioned themselves for planned attacks later one. I guess at that point, though, being on the line was normal for them; it was 'home'."

"As far George's remarks about wishing for the kind of food you could only get back home… Can't you just picture it; a bunch of tired, dirty, homesick soldiers sitting around talking about the things they missed most about home?"

"I can just hear George bragging about Mom's fried chicken and hot rolls, or tomatoes and cucumbers out of the garden, or Inah's pies. Then the next guy would chime in about his wife's blackberry cobbler, and then someone else would brag about their grandma's baked ham, and on and on it would go until they fell silent; lost in their own personal thoughts of home and family."

"I want to take a minute to put a few things into perspective here. First of all, George wrote that they had received their cots and clean clothing only two days before writing this letter on February 16th. Happy Valentine's Day to them!"

"Secondly, what makes this so note-worthy is the fact that they arrived on Luzon on January 9th. That means that for over a month, these guys slept on the ground and wore the same clothes, socks and underwear the entire time."

"Not only did they endure these conditions for over a month, but history tells us that when George's unit arrived on the shores of Luzon, they fought their way to shore and deeper into the island. Do you understand what this means? This means that these boys lived, worked, ate, and slept in clothes that were wet, sandy, sweaty, and dirty. George and the other medics (and I'm sure other guys) didn't get to stop there, though. In addition to their own body odor, sand, water, and mud, they wore the blood and who knows what else of the wounded and dead they treated. Not a very pleasant thought, to say the least. But they did it and they did it for me. For you. For all of us."

"Rotation was as uncertain as anything else in those days. Just think about what we hear on the news now; troops deployed, and troops withdrawn. Nobody could predict with 100% certainty what the enemy was going to do then any more than they can now. But George had been gone for so long…hadn't the army had him long enough? He had a family who needed and wanted him back so badly. He had a little brother who wanted him around to help him grow up to be a man."

"Reading George's letters after all these years has caused me to recall memories of places, people and events I had not thought of in years."

"One of the most vivid memories being how excited I got whenever George wrote that he thought he would be home by fall. I remember I started rattling off a list of things I wanted the two of us to do. Dad and Mom laughed and said doing all of that would make him more tired than all the fighting he'd been doing. Then they warned me about not getting my hopes up too high-that what George said may only have been his wishful thinking."

"I know now that their warning was as much for themselves as it was for me. But even now I think about what if he'd have been one of the lucky few to have left. What if he would have been the one guy that left in February?"

"He felt certain he'd be home before fall. You know what they say…there are no certainties in war."

"It sounds a little crazy to read what he wrote about how pretty the island was and wanting to see more of it. The welcome wagon had not been the ones to greet them when they came ashore. So why would he write something like this?"

"As it turns out, they were in a holding pattern at this point and for all practical purposes, you could say they were alone. I'm not sure what George and his fellow soldiers thought was going on, but I have the advantage of being able to read what was happening all these years later. I have to remind myself that when George wrote this letter he was unaware of their mistaken route** and what was eventually in store for them."

"I'm glad he didn't know then what I know now. I'm glad and thankful they were able to rest and relax for a while. Most of all, I am beyond thankful that George could still see the beauty in things-that his heart and mind had not become hard. I am thankful that he unwittingly let us know this about him by wanting to share what he was seeing with us."

"As for George being as safe there as he was at home, I am uncertain as to what he was trying to convey. Did he have a false sense of security?"

"Was it a poor but sincere attempt to reassure our family? I don't know. But I do know: 1. We knew George was somewhere in the South Pacific 2. Thanks to Armed Forces Radio and the Associated Press, we knew what was going on over there and 3. George couldn't have been more wrong."

FYI

On January 9th, 1945, the 43rd was part of a huge amphibious landing on Luzon-the largest of the Philippine Islands. Their goal was to take back control of the island from the Japanese. General Douglas McArthur had been waiting for the opportunity to take back this island since the Japanese had taken control of Luzon in December of 1941.

George was one of 175,000 soldiers who would be going against over 260,000 Japanese to accomplish what would prove to be a grueling and costly task. The fact that the Japanese outnumbered the Americans was not something McArthur worried about. The Japanese, on the other hand, did.

The Japanese knew that the fact that they outnumbered their enemy did not change the fact that they were inferior in the areas of weapons, transport, and modern equipment. Their hope and intention was to put up minimal resistance in the harbors and airfields and concentrate their efforts in the field. Three mountain strongholds-one in particular-the Ipo Dam was the main water source for the highly populated city of Manila and where the Japanese were prepared to fight body for body to the bloody end.

The day George wrote this letter was probably a fairly quiet one. After the initial bloody and combative arrival on the island, their unit was in a holding pattern. While other units were battling for control of Manila and other key points, they were waiting for their next move further into the mountains....

In regard to George's reference to clean clothes...

The military did what they could to make things as clean and comfortable as possible, but the U.S. military isn't in the business of clean and comfortable.

They are in the business of defeating the enemy; and enemy that didn't wait for kitchens and camps to be built before trying to strike. That is why instruction in personal hygiene was (and still is) as much a part of a soldier's training as combat readiness.

Getting that set of clean clothes and a cot to sleep in were what could easily be described as essential luxuries. It was *essential* for a solider to be as careful and fastidious about his personal hygiene as humanly possible under the circumstances while at the same time, a *luxury* for being able to do so.

The military had learned from experience in previous wars, however, that these essential luxuries could possibly mean the difference between victory and defeat. That is why in preparation for going overseas, a soldier was instructed and trained in how to prevent head and body lice, foot rot, trench foot, dysentery, and malaria.

Medics like George, as well as the doctors and nurses in the field hospitals During WWII, had more than enough to do in trying to care for the wounded — often times in rudimentary make-shift hospitals without the proper equipment and medications. They did not need the added burden of a lice-infested camp, or soldiers unable to walk due to foot rot. For these reasons, soldiers were encouraged to bathe as often as possible, wash their socks and always...ALWAYS keep their feet dry whenever possible.

As if wet, dirty, and primitive conditions weren't enough, diseases such as malaria were almost as big an enemy as the Axis powers and Japan.

In fact, the military admits that malaria reduced the number of capable fighting men in many military units fighting in the South Pacific and Philippines by as much as 75% at times.

These staggering statistics are why other regular reminders (orders) to soldiers included being ready to use the issued sulfa powder and pills when or if necessary and to use the d insect replant and mosquito netting.

But who had the time and resources to do laundry? Certainly not a soldier. Besides, laundry facilities on the battlefield were about as feasible as weekend passes to go home. That's where the local natives and residents George wrote about proved to be helpful.

The people indigenous to the lands used as battle fields oftentimes took the entrepreneurial route by offering laundry and sewing services, food, drink, knick-knacks and even entertainment to the troops for a reasonable price. These things were welcomed by the soldiers and allowed us to get on with the business of the war and (for the most part) established good relationships between the two groups of people.

Besides, it was the least we could 'do' considering...

The influx of American and Allied soldiers on foreign soil-especially the islands-created complete and utter chaos to the native residents of places the majority of people in America and Europe had never even heard of.

Their once tranquil and undisturbed lifestyles were replaced with destruction, death, and all other sorts of ugliness. Their lifestyles and cultures were invaded and often times their lands were confiscated for the war effort.

Soldiers who were frustrated and suffering from emotional and mental fatigue were guilty on several occasions, of taking advantage of the young women where they were at. Whether by force, by promising to love them forever or by playing on their emotions (give a soldier who may die tomorrow something to remember), the fact is that over 2,000 babies born to women in the South Pacific fathered by American soldiers during World War II. So in spite of us being the 'good guys', we were still outsiders--intruders who came, conquered and left…leaving more behind than we should have….

At this point the 43rd was resting; they were in a holding pattern in the hillsides of Luzon east of Manila (details to follow). Meanwhile the 34th Infantry, portions of the 38th Division and the 503rd Parachute Regimental Combat team were battling for Bataan and Corregidor and the 11th Airborne, 1st Cavalry, the 37th division along with other smaller units were driving the Japanese from Manila.

Japan's General Yamashita really didn't care about Manila. Knowing he was not equipped to defend Manila, his plan was to blow up bridges and other vital points to cripple the city and evacuate before American troops got there on February 4th, 1945.

Japanese Rear Admiral Sanji, Japanese naval commander for the area, had other ideas, however. Vowing to fight to the last man, intense battle lasted almost a month. McArthur was genuinely concerned about the civilian population in the area and did his best to keep them safe by enforcing strict curfews and rules for their safety. But these things could only do so much. The devastation was widespread. Once Manila was secured, we were able to refocus our efforts to the outlying mountain areas where George and the others were waiting.

**Lt. General Walter Krueger was given the responsibility by General McArthur of leading troops through the mountainous hillsides of Luzon to secure Manila's water supply which came from the Angat and Marikina Rivers. But Krueger was mistakenly leading them to the WaWa Dam which had been abandoned in 1938.

It was two months before he realized the error and turned them toward Ipo Dam in the Marikina Valley. This, combined with a critical erroneous intelligence report underestimating Japanese troops by 10,000, caused serious time delays and allowed the Japanese to lengthen and strengthen their line of defense.

On March 13, 1945, the 43rd arrived to assist the troops already there in securing a strong foothold on Mt. Mataba in order to preserve Ipo Dam. But by the end of the next day over 300 American soldiers had given their lives and over 1000 more were wounded.

March 13, 1945 Luzon

Dear Dad,

It is really a beautiful cool morning. Before the day is over, though, it will be plenty hot.

Haven't received any mail lately, some should be in today.

Have seen most of the island but haven't had enough time on a few occasions. There is a very beautiful view from here. Our chow is good as we are eating from the kitchen.

How is school, Benny? Won't be long until school is out, will it?

Not much of a letter I know, but something to tell you I am ok.

All my love,
George

"History tells me that this was the day George went into combat-an ongoing battle that would end up costing George his life. In addition to the fighting, George was among the medics who cared for the one thousand 'plus' who were wounded and who probably tried to save at least a few of the three hundred who died that day."

"I have no proof, but every ounce of my being tells me he wrote this letter just in case it would be his last. Time just didn't permit him to write more than he did. George didn't want to come out and actually tell us this may be his last letter. He would never have done that to us. But George being George, he wanted to give us something. He even made sure I had a little something of my own. He did that a lot and I always felt really proud when Mom or Dad would read those parts of George's letters to me."

"I might be searching a bit, but I also feel like this letter is a bit cryptic. I think his mention of it getting really hot by the end of the day was about a lot more than the actual temperature. What stands out to me even more is the fact that he made the reference to it almost being time for school to be out. In March? George knew better than that! Say whatever you want, but I am convinced that this is his way of trying to tell us that their position was intense and that they were hoping or looking forward to it being over very soon."

"Oh, how I wish it wouldn't have been over so soon for George. "

Mar 16, 1945, Luzon

Dear Dad,

Have been taking it quite easy lately. Have lots to write about, but censorship won't pass so this will be just a note to let you know I'm alright.

Our chow is swell. Meals from the kitchen, and the field rations are tops.

Nothing new on rotation. Still planning and praying to be home by end of summer.

How about a note, Benny?

Tell everyone hello.

All my love,

George

"This is the last letter George wrote home. Exactly one week later he would be killed in action. Exactly one week later, the war department would be writing to my family to express their condolences and offer what they thought would bring a sense of pride and closure to our family after two and a half years of waiting for George's return."

"The letter was short, but it spoke volumes about George's final days. He wrote that he had so much he wanted to tell us but couldn't. I know from this statement (and history books) that George had been involved in some of the war's most fierce battles to that point and week that followed this letter would be even worse. But the battle at Luzon was also a decisive turning point in the war. After this battle the Japanese knew they didn't stand a chance."

"George said the food was great. There is definitely a chance that his definition of 'great food' was somewhat different that it was when he left home, but there is also the chance that the food was actually good"

"It doesn't really matter. What does matter is that he was satisfied and felt that the needs of the soldiers were being met."

"His last written request was for me to write him a letter. My brother George wanted a letter from me — a fourteen-year-old boy who wrote about school and friends and the comings and goings of our small town. He wanted a letter from the fourteen-year-old boy fortunate enough to be able to call him brother. I never wrote the letter he asked for because seven days later, on March 23rd, 1945, in the final push up the mountain to claim the island of Luzon away from the Japanese, Technician Third Grade, George E. Burks, 37,208,034, Medical Department, was killed in action. I never wrote the letter George asked for because we received word of his death before we got his letter asking me to write him."

"There are so many things I wish I could have told him. I wish I could have told him I was going to college after I graduated from high school. I wish I could tell have told him I was going to the army after I finished two years of college. I wish I could have told him I fell in love with, and married a girl named Betty. I wish I could have told him when I was going to be a father. I wish I could have told him when I was going to be a grandfather."

"In other words, I wish I could have shared my life with my older brother because he was the kind of guy who would have wanted to be there for all of it."

"I don't have to wish I could have told George how much I loved him, though, because I did. I told him every time I wrote him how much I loved him."

"My name is Grover Bentley "Benny" Burks and my brother died in World War II. He died defending our country's freedom. He died fighting alongside and caring for the wounded and dying. He died a hero; his heroic actions being recognized and decorated."

"That's all very well and good, but it doesn't change the fact that George died. It doesn't change the fact that my twelve-year-old self told my brother goodbye and never got the chance to say 'welcome home'."

"I hope my words have not taken away from the historical value of George's letters. Instead, I hope my words have added to their value by giving you a deeper appreciation for the extreme sacrifices families make who give one of their own for our country. I hope George's letters and my words will make you more sensitive to your patriotic duty; supporting the soldiers and their families who are called to serve-no matter what your political views are. I hope you never forget to remember heroes like my brother George. I know never will."

Letters from officers of the U.S. Army

April 21, 1945

(telegram from the Adjutant General)

The secretary of war desires me to express his deepest regret that your son Tec/3 Burks, George E was killed in action on Luzon 23 Mar 45 Confirming letter follows.

Ulio, The Adjutant General

April 23, 194

Dear Mr. Burks

It is with regret that I am writing to confirm the recent telegram informing you of the death of your son, Technician Third Grade, George E. Burks, 37, 208,034, Medical Department, who was killed in action on 23 March 1945 on Luzon Island, Philippine Islands.

I fully understand your desire to learn as much as possible regarding the circumstances leading to his death. Recently provisions were made whereby there will be sent directly to the emergency addressee or the next of kin a letter containing further information about each person who dies overseas in the service of our country, and if this letter has not already been received, it may be expected soon. I know the sorrow this message has brought you and it is my hope that in time the knowledge of his heroic service to his country, even unto death, may be of sustaining comfort to you.

I extend to you my deepest sympathy.

Sincerely yours,

J.A. Ulio, Major General, The Adjutant General

(Letter signed by Douglas MacArthur)

May 4, 1945

Dear Mr. Burks:

My deepest sympathy goes to you in the death of your son, Technician Third Grade George E. Burks.

Your consolation for his loss may be that he died in the service of his country in a just cause and for the benefit of all.

Very faithfully,
Douglas MacArthur

FYI

It is interesting to note that General MacArthur did not sign his name using his official title, but rather simply Douglas MacArthur.

Closing thoughts

From the day my Dad showed me the box that held Uncle George's letters I have grown as a person and as an American citizen in many, many ways.

George Burks is now much more than just a name I heard from time to time. He's Dad's brother, my uncle and a young man who gave his life for the life of freedom and beauty we all enjoy today. He was a young man who wasn't afraid or embarrassed to invest himself into the lives of those he loved. As I held each letter in my hand, I realized what an intimate piece of history I was holding. Reading the words written with so much love by the man I came to know and love, I was able to see him for who he was-kind, gentle, sincere, humorous, strong, selfless, and brave. I am humbled and honored to call him family.

The grave marker bearing his name in the cemetery in Crocker, MO is now more than just a piece of rock I helped place flowers in front of each Memorial Day as a child. It is my family's memorial to their son/brother-marking the place a hero was sacrificially laid to rest.

I am now more knowledgeable of the events of World War II known as the South Pacific Theater. My geography skills have been honed and I have a much firmer grasp on the 'who, what, where, how and why' of the events that took place there during the war.

My pride in my country has also been restored. Considering the near absence of morals, integrity, and sense of responsibility in America today, this was a humbling and somber reminder of who we used to be and who I believe we can be once again. It gives me hope.

For Uncle George, the letters he wrote were a way to stay in touch; to stay connected with the people he loved while he was so far from home. That's all.

I'm sure it never entered his mind that someday his letters would be the catalyst for creating an awareness of what it is like to be that younger brother and sister left behind to wait…worry…grieve.

Thank you, Dad, for opening your heart and your life to me in a way I would never have imagined was there.

Thank you, Uncle George, for, well, for everything. I only wish we could have known each other, because I am certain my life would be richer for it.

George E. Burks

The picture of George Benny put in the high school yearbook

George and Betty Edwards in Auckland, New Zealand

George and some of the other soldiers in his regiment with a
Japanese flag they retrieved after battle. George is in the very
back just to the left of the soldier holding the left-hand corner
of the flag.

Grave marker for George E. Burks in cemetery #1 in Manila

Grave marker for George E. Burks in Crocker, MO

Darla Noble is an author and speaker specializing in inspirational nonfiction, historical nonfiction, and Christian devotionals. For more information about Darla's books, visit her website:

www.dnoblewrites.com

Made in the USA
Monee, IL
05 June 2022